COMPASSIONATE CARE: ACCEPTING THE DEMENTIA DIAGNOSIS

EMPOWERING CHOICES AND ENHANCING QUALITY OF LIFE THROUGH EARLY INTERVENTION

L.E. SUMMERS

CONTENTS

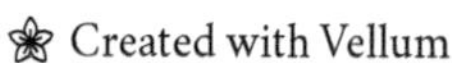 Created with Vellum

To my dearest mother,

This book is a tribute to your unwavering strength and the love that flowed through you. As I delve through the depths of dementia, I am reminded of our journey together—the highs and lows, the moments of confusion and clarity, and the unbreakable bond we shared.

You faced the relentless grip of dementia with courage and grace, teaching me the true meaning of resilience. Through your unwavering spirit, you taught me the power of embracing each day, no matter how challenging it became. Your steadfast love and determination inspired me to embark on this journey of understanding, to shed light on the complexities of dementia.

In this book, I strive to honor your memory and the countless others who have faced this formidable foe. By sharing our story, I hope to offer solace, guidance, and a glimmer of hope to those who are navigating this path.

Mom, your legacy lives on in every word of this book. You may have been taken from us by dementia's grip, but your spirit endures in my heart. Through this book, I hope to raise awareness to help bring a world where no one faces dementia alone.

This dedication is a testament to the extraordinary woman you were— a beacon of love, strength, and resilience. Thank you for the indelible mark you left on my life, and may your light shine brightly, illuminating the path for others who face the challenges of dementia.

I will always love you, Mom.

I also would like to take a moment to thank those people in my life who have helped me in my endeavor to write my books on the subject of dementia caregiving—a special thanks to my wonderful children, Miles and Tyler, and to their mother, Iseabail Lane. I don't think I could have done any of this without their support.

INTRODUCTION

Life is full of unexpected turns, and for me, one of the most challenging was becoming my mother's caregiver as she battled dementia. For three and a half years, I watched as the woman who had always been my rock, my confidante, and my source of unwavering love and support slowly slipped away. Her once-sharp mind, filled with stories and wisdom, became clouded by this relentless disease, and each day brought new challenges, new losses, and a growing sense of helplessness. It was heart-breaking, exhausting, and often overwhelming, but it was also a journey filled with unexpected moments of grace, love, and resilience.

This book isn't a medical textbook or a dry recitation of dementia facts and figures. It's a heartfelt story about my mom, the woman who taught me the meaning of strength, compassion, and unconditional love. It's about the raw emotions that bubbled up within me, the difficult decisions I had to make, and the small victories that felt like beacons of light in the darkest of times. It's about learning to let go of the past and embrace the present, finding joy in the simplest of moments, and discovering a deeper connection with my mother, even as her memories faded.

My mother was born a central Texas girl who loved collecting dolls and eating licorice. Her mother was a schoolteacher who first taught in a one-room schoolhouse and even had a school named after her. Her father was an officer in the Border Patrol and later became a US Customs agent. My mom was an excellent student (her mother ensured that) and took every chance she had to cook. She had two younger brothers who she loved dearly. When she met my father, he was a lineman for the telephone company and would call her from atop a telephone pole. They soon married, and two years later, I was born, and later my sister came along. My mother was a Renaissance woman who made a happy home. She was a wonder with ceramics and pottery, sewing prom dresses, and taking exotic cooking and pastry classes. When her memory started fading, and things just weren't quite right, it was so hard for her family to accept. However, acceptance is the key to moving forward and doing the best in all concerns.

When my mom was first diagnosed, I felt lost. The world of dementia was unfamiliar and frightening. I didn't know where to turn or how to handle the challenges that lay ahead. However, I slowly began to find my way through many hours of research, conversations with healthcare professionals who became trusted advisors, and the unwavering support of other caregivers who understood my struggles. I learned about the importance of early diagnosis, the different stages of the disease, and the various treatment options available. I discovered resources and strategies I never knew existed and found comfort in knowing I wasn't alone on this journey.

But the most important lesson I learned was the power of acceptance. I was accepting the diagnosis, accepting the changes in my mom, and accepting the limitations of my own abilities as a caregiver. It wasn't easy, but it was liberating. It allowed me to let go of the guilt, the anger, and the frustration and to be present with my mom in each moment. It allowed me to focus on what truly mattered: cherishing the time we had left together and creating meaningful moments amid the confusion.

In this book, I'll share the knowledge I gained, the strategies I used, and the stories that touched my heart. I'll talk about the practical aspects of caregiving, from managing medications and daily routines to dealing with challenging behaviors and ensuring safety. But I'll also share the emotional side of the journey, the grief, the guilt, the fear, and the moments of happiness that made it seem not so bad. I'll share the intimate moments, the inside jokes, the shared tears, and the quiet moments of understanding that transcended words.

By sharing my story, I hope to offer comfort and support to other caregivers feeling overwhelmed and alone. I want you to know that you're not alone, that resources are available to help you, and that even in the darkest times, there is always hope to be found. This book is dedicated to my mom, the strongest woman I've ever known, and to all the caregivers who give so much of themselves to love and care for others. In the next chapter, I will start by setting the groundwork related to dementia types and stages.

Gift Offer

I want to thank you so much for choosing this book, and I hope you will find it informative and supportive, but most of all compassionate. In hopes of enhancing your navigation, I am offering some complementary items that I think you will find valuable in your care journey. In addition, I would like to send you a periodic newsletter that I hope you will find helpful.

To receive your gift items, scan the QR code using your phone or tablet, or enter the link in your browser.

Or,

CompassionateCare.fyi/get-my-gift

Please enjoy the book!

Thank you,

L.E. Summers

THE FUNDAMENTALS OF DEMENTIA

Dementia isn't a single disease but a broad term for conditions affecting brain function, primarily memory, thinking, and reasoning. Imagine it is like a tree with many branches, each representing a different type of dementia. While distinct in their origins and manifestations, these branches all lead to a decline in a person's ability to think, remember, and reason clearly. It is essential for caregivers and families to understand these various types and their distinct symptoms to provide the most appropriate care and support.

The most prevalent branch on this metaphorical tree is Alzheimer's disease, accounting for 60-80% (Alzheimer's Association 2023) of all dementia cases. This progressive neurodegenerative disease typically starts with subtle memory lapses and gradually worsens over time, impacting language, problem-solving, and, eventually, essential daily functions.

Another significant branch is vascular dementia, estimated to affect 10-20% of individuals with dementia. It's caused by reduced blood flow to the brain, often because of strokes or other vascular problems. Unlike the gradual decline seen in

Alzheimer's, vascular dementia can progress in a step manner, with sudden changes in cognitive function followed by periods of stability. Common symptoms include difficulty with attention, planning, decision-making (National Institutes of Health, 2021), and physical symptoms like weakness or numbness.

Lewy body dementia, affecting 5-15% of individuals with dementia, is characterized by Lewy bodies abnormal protein deposits found throughout the brain. These deposits disrupt the brain's normal operations, leading to a wide range of symptoms. Cognitive fluctuations, where the person's alertness and attention vary significantly daily or even hour to hour, are a hallmark of Lewy body dementia. Other common symptoms include visual hallucinations, sleep disturbances, and movement difficulties that are like those seen in Parkinson's disease.

Frontotemporal dementia, a less common type but still significant, primarily affects the frontal and temporal lobes of the brain, which handle personality, behavior, and language. This type of dementia often strikes earlier in life, typically between the ages of 45 and 65. The most notable symptoms include changes in personality, social behavior, and language abilities, such as difficulty finding words or understanding speech.

Mixed dementia occurs when a person has more than one type of dementia, such as Alzheimer's disease and vascular dementia. This type can be particularly challenging to diagnose and manage, as the symptoms can vary widely depending on the combination of underlying diseases.

Understanding the different types of dementia is just the first step. Recognizing the common symptoms and how they progress over time is equally important. In the early stages, the signs can be subtle and easily dismissed as normal aging. Forgetfulness, difficulty finding words, misplacing items, and changes in mood or personality are all common early indicators.

As dementia progresses, these symptoms worsen, affecting various aspects of a person's life. Memory loss becomes more pronounced, making it difficult to recall recent events or even the names of loved ones. Difficulty with language can lead to communication breakdowns and frustration. Changes in mood and behavior can appear as increased anxiety, agitation, depression, or even paranoia. In the later stages, the person may need help with basic activities of daily living, such as bathing, dressing, and eating. They may also have trouble walking, swallowing, and communicating their needs.

Recognizing the signs and understanding how dementia progresses is crucial for caregivers and families to provide the proper care and support. While there is no cure for dementia, early diagnosis, and intervention can make a significant difference in managing symptoms, improving quality of life, and allowing individuals to maintain their independence for as long as possible.

THE SCIENCE BEHIND DEMENTIA: WHAT HAPPENS IN THE BRAIN

Dementia isn't just a condition of the mind; it's a disease of the brain. To understand it better, we need to dive into the complex world of neuroscience and explore the changes that occur within this vital organ. This knowledge isn't meant to overwhelm but to empower. By understanding the science behind dementia, we can approach it with greater compassion, develop more effective care strategies, and advocate for research that may one day lead to a cure.

The brain is a remarkable organ, a network of billions of nerve cells, or neurons, that communicate with each other through electrical and chemical signals. These intricate connections allow us to think, feel, remember, and experience the world around us. In dementia, these connections become disrupted, leading to a gradual decline in cognitive function.

Let's take a closer look at the science behind some of the most common types of dementia:

- <u>Alzheimer's disease</u>: In this neurodegenerative disorder, two abnormal structures called amyloid plaques and tau tangles accumulate in the brain. Amyloid plaques are sticky clumps of protein that build up between nerve cells, interfering with their communication. Tau tangles are twisted fibers of another protein called tau, which form inside neurons and disrupt their internal transport systems. Over time, these changes cause widespread damage to the brain, leading to the common symptoms of Alzheimer's, such as memory loss, confusion, and difficulty with everyday tasks.
- <u>Vascular dementia</u>: This type of dementia is caused by reduced blood flow to the brain, often due to strokes or other vascular problems. Think of it like a city with damaged roads and traffic jams; the essential nutrients and oxygen carried by blood can't reach their destinations efficiently. This deprivation can cause brain cells to die, particularly in areas responsible for memory and executive function, leading to cognitive decline.
- <u>Lewy body dementia</u>: This complex form of dementia shares characteristics with both Alzheimer's and Parkinson's disease. It's named after the Lewy bodies, abnormal protein deposits that can be found throughout the brain in people with this condition. These deposits interfere with the production and function of various neurotransmitters, including

dopamine and acetylcholine, which are essential for
movement, thinking, and memory. This disruption
leads to a unique set of symptoms, including
fluctuations in cognitive function, visual hallucinations,
and motor problems.

- <u>Frontotemporal dementia</u>: As the name suggests, this
type primarily affects the frontal and temporal lobes of
the brain, regions responsible for personality, behavior,
and language. This type often strikes earlier in life,
typically between the ages of 45 and 65. The underlying
causes can vary but usually involve accumulating
abnormal proteins in these brain regions.

Regardless of the specific type of dementia, the result is the
same: a progressive decline in brain function and a loss of
cognitive abilities. The areas of the brain responsible for
memory, language, problem-solving, and decision-making are
particularly vulnerable. As these areas become damaged, the
symptoms of dementia become more apparent.

While the science behind dementia can seem daunting, it's
important to remember that research is constantly evolving.
Scientists are continually working to unravel the complexities
of this disease, exploring new avenues for treatment and
prevention. By staying informed about the latest research, we
can not only better understand dementia but also advocate for
increased funding and resources to support those affected by
this devastating condition.

EARLY SIGNS OF DEMENTIA: BEYOND
FORGETFULNESS

Early detection of dementia is critical to benefit both the individual and their caregivers. It's like noticing a faint wisp of
smoke before a fire erupts—timely intervention can make all

the difference. However, dementia's early signs can be subtle, often masked by the normal aging process or other health conditions. It requires a keen eye, a compassionate heart, and a willingness to confront the possibility that something more serious may be at play.

While memory loss is often the most well-known symptom of dementia, it's crucial to remember that it's not the only one. In fact, dementia can manifest in a myriad of ways, affecting different parts of the brain and impacting daily life in subtle yet significant ways. These early signs may vary depending on the type of dementia and the individual's unique circumstances. However, there are some common red flags that caregivers and loved ones should be vigilant about:

- <u>Memory loss that disrupts daily life</u>: Forgetting recently learned information, important dates, or events.
- <u>Challenges in planning or solving problems</u>: Difficulty completing familiar tasks, following a recipe, or working with numbers.
- <u>Confusion with time or place</u>: Losing track of dates, seasons, or getting lost in familiar places.
- <u>Difficulty understanding visual images and spatial relationships</u>: Trouble reading, judging distance, or determining color or contrast.
- <u>New problems with words in speaking or writing</u>: Difficulty following or joining a conversation, needing help finding the right words, or repeating themselves.
- <u>Decreased or poor judgment</u>: Making questionable decisions, neglecting personal hygiene, or showing poor financial judgment.
- <u>Withdrawal from work or social activities</u>: Losing interest in hobbies, avoiding social interactions, or having difficulty keeping up with a favorite sports team.

- <u>Changes in mood and personality</u>: Becoming confused, suspicious, depressed, fearful, or anxious.

These changes can be subtle at first, but they can gradually worsen over time. If you notice any of these signs in yourself or a loved one, it's crucial to consult with a doctor as soon as possible. While dismissing these changes as a normal part of aging can be tempting, early diagnosis is essential for accessing appropriate treatment and support.

Early detection of dementia opens the door to a range of interventions that can help manage symptoms, slow down the progression of the disease, and improve the quality of life for both the individual and their caregivers. It allows timely access to medications, therapies, and support services that can make a significant difference in the long run.

Remember, early diagnosis is not a death sentence. It's an opportunity to take control, make informed decisions, and plan for the future. It's about empowering yourself and your loved ones to live the best possible life, even in the face of this challenging disease.

THE IMPORTANCE OF EARLY DIAGNOSIS: CHANGING THE COURSE

Imagine dementia as a river, its currents growing stronger and more treacherous as it flows downstream. Early diagnosis is like building a dam upstream, redirecting the flow, and creating a calmer, more manageable environment. While we can't stop the river entirely, we can significantly influence its course and slow the potential damage it can cause.

Early diagnosis of dementia is not a moment of despair but rather a turning point, an opportunity to take proactive steps and shape the journey ahead. It's about empowering individuals and their families with knowledge, resources, and a sense of control in the face of an uncertain future.

One of the most significant advantages of early diagnosis is access to timely treatment and support services. With dementia, time is of the essence. Research has shown that early intervention can slow down the progression of the disease, alleviate symptoms, and improve overall quality of life. Medications, therapies, and lifestyle modifications can all play a role in managing dementia effectively, but their impact is often most significant when started early.

Early diagnosis also allows individuals and their families to make informed decisions about future care. This includes discussions about living arrangements, healthcare wishes, and financial planning. By having these conversations early on, while cognitive function remains relatively intact, individuals can express their preferences and ensure their wishes are respected as the disease progresses. This proactive planning can alleviate stress and uncertainty for both the individual and their loved ones.

Another crucial benefit of early diagnosis is the opportunity to make lifestyle changes that can positively impact cognitive function. Research shows that a healthy diet, regular exercise, social interaction, and brain stimulation can all play a role in slowing the progression of dementia and maintaining brain health. By identifying dementia early on, individuals can adopt these lifestyle modifications and potentially delay the onset of more severe symptoms.

Early diagnosis may also open the door for some individuals to participate in clinical trials. These trials are essential for developing new treatments and therapies for dementia. By participating in a clinical trial, individuals can access potentially beneficial interventions and contribute to research that may ultimately help others.

Finally, early diagnosis can reduce anxiety and uncertainty. Receiving a diagnosis can be overwhelming, but it also provides clarity and direction. By knowing what they are facing, individuals and their families can educate themselves about dementia, connect with support groups, and develop coping mechanisms to navigate the challenges ahead. This knowledge can empower them to take control of the situation, make informed decisions, and focus on maximizing quality of life.

Early diagnosis is not about giving up or accepting defeat. It's about taking a proactive approach, embracing the journey with knowledge and hope, and creating a roadmap for the future. It's about cherishing the present moment, celebrating the individual's strengths and abilities, and finding meaning and purpose in the face of adversity. By seizing the opportunity of early diagnosis, we can change the course of dementia and create a more supportive and empowering experience for everyone involved.

COGNITIVE TESTS EXPLAINED: UNDERSTANDING THE DIAGNOSTIC PROCESS

The process of a dementia diagnosis can be a daunting one, filled with uncertainty and apprehension. However, it's important to remember that a diagnosis is not an end but rather a new beginning—a starting point for understanding, planning, and seeking support.

Cognitive tests play a crucial role in diagnosis. These tests are not designed to trick or confuse but rather to assess an individual's mental abilities, providing valuable insights into their brain function. Think of them as a flashlight illuminating the inner workings of the mind, revealing areas that may be affected by dementia.

- <u>Mini-Mental State Examination (MMSE)</u>: This widely used test assesses orientation, attention, memory, language, and visuospatial skills. It is a quick and easy screening tool to help identify individuals needing further evaluation.
- <u>Montreal Cognitive Assessment (MoCA)</u>: This more comprehensive test evaluates a broader range of cognitive functions, including executive function, attention, language, memory, abstraction, and orientation. The MoCA is often used when the MMSE results are inconclusive or when a more detailed assessment is needed to pinpoint specific areas of cognitive impairment.
- <u>Neuropsychological testing</u>: This in-depth evaluation is conducted by a neuropsychologist, a specialist trained in assessing brain function. Neuropsychological testing involves a series of tests that measure various cognitive domains, such as memory, attention, language, executive function, processing speed, and visuospatial skills. This comprehensive assessment can provide a detailed profile of an individual's cognitive strengths and weaknesses, aiding in diagnosis and treatment planning.

It's important to understand that cognitive tests are not foolproof. Factors like anxiety, fatigue, or cultural background can influence performance. Additionally, some individuals with mild cognitive impairment or early-stage dementia may perform well on these tests, masking the underlying condition. Therefore, cognitive tests are just one piece of the puzzle. Healthcare professionals also consider the individual's medical history, neurological exams, and other relevant factors to arrive at a diagnosis.

If you or a loved one is undergoing cognitive testing, it's essential to approach it with an open mind and a willingness to learn. These tests can provide valuable information about cognitive function, helping to identify areas of concern and guide treatment decisions. They can also offer reassurance, ruling out other potential causes of cognitive decline and confirming a diagnosis.

Remember, a dementia diagnosis is not a definitive end. It's a starting point for understanding, seeking support, and planning for the future. Cognitive tests can help us navigate this journey, providing valuable insights into brain health and empowering us to make informed decisions about care and treatment.

DEBUNKING THE MYTHS: SEPARATING FACT FROM FICTION

Dementia is often surrounded by a lot of misconceptions and half-truths that can be a source of confusion and fear for those facing a diagnosis or caring for a loved one with the condition (Alzheimer's Association, 2023). It's time to shine a light on the truth, dispelling the myths perpetuating stigma and misunderstanding. Let's delve into ten common misconceptions about dementia and illuminate the reality behind them.

Myth 1: Dementia is a normal part of aging.

Fact: While cognitive decline can occur with age, dementia is not a natural consequence of aging. It's a disease process that affects the brain, causing significant impairment in memory, thinking, and behavior.

Myth 2: Memory loss is the only symptom of dementia.

> Fact: Dementia encompasses a wide array of symptoms, including difficulties with language, problem-solving, judgment, personality changes, and even hallucinations. Memory loss is a prominent feature but not the only indicator.

Myth 3: There is no treatment for dementia.

> Fact: While there's no cure for dementia, there are treatments and interventions that can manage symptoms, slow progression, and improve quality of life. Medications, therapies, lifestyle modifications, and supportive care can all make a positive difference.

Myth 4: People with dementia are incapable of enjoying life.

> Fact: Dementia doesn't rob individuals of their emotions or their ability to experience joy and connection. Even in the later stages, they can still appreciate music, nature, humor, and the love of those around them.

Myth 5: Dementia only affects older people.

> Fact: Although dementia is more common in older adults, it can also affect younger individuals. Early-onset dementia can occur in people as young as their 30s or 40s.

Myth 6: Dementia is always hereditary.

> Fact: While genetics can play a role in some types of dementia, especially early-onset Alzheimer's, most cases are not directly inherited. Lifestyle factors, cardiovascular health, and other environmental influences also contribute.

Myth 7: People with dementia are dangerous and violent.

Fact: Aggression and agitation can sometimes occur in dementia, but it's not a universal experience. These behaviors can often be managed effectively with understanding, patience, and appropriate support.

Myth 8: Once someone has dementia, there's nothing they can do to help themselves.

Fact: Lifestyle modifications, such as a healthy diet, regular exercise, and cognitive stimulation, can have a positive impact on brain health and may even slow the progression of dementia.

Myth 9: Dementia is a mental illness.

Fact: Dementia is a neurological disorder, not a mental illness. It's caused by physical changes in the brain that affect cognitive function.

Myth 10: People with dementia are burdens on their families and society.

Fact: People with dementia deserve love, respect, and support. They are valuable members of our communities, and their contributions should be acknowledged and appreciated.

By dispelling these myths and embracing the truths about dementia, we can foster a more compassionate and understanding society. We can empower individuals with dementia to live fulfilling lives, support their caregivers, and advocate for increased research and resources to combat this challenging disease.

Remember, the dementia patient is not giving you a hard time. The dementia patient is having a hard time. - Teepa Snow, dementia care expert

CHAPTER 1 PRACTICAL EXERCISE

I would like to encourage you to start a journal as you begin your caregiving journey. Consider it to be your safe space to write down your thoughts and feelings along the way. There is great value in exploring your thoughts, feelings and experiences both at the present time and in the future as reflections of your experience and growth. There are no correct answers. I will provide some starting points for your journal, but feel free to use the journal to your best benefit.

1. How do I feel today?
2. What valuable lessons did I learn today?
3. Where did I find joy or satisfaction?
4. What was a challenge that I faced today?
5. Did I share my experiences or emotions with someone today?
6. What did I learn about myself today?

Get a new diary or grab a notebook just for these reflections. Set a reminder for the end of the day to help you remember to write down your thoughts. This will be a valuable tool in making you the best caregiver that you can be.

NAVIGATING THE EMOTIONAL JOURNEY

The journey of dementia caregiving often begins with a diagnosis, a moment that can shatter the world as you know it. It's a moment filled with shock, disbelief, and a whirlwind of emotions that can leave you feeling lost and overwhelmed. But within this initial turmoil lies the seed of acceptance, a powerful force that can transform your experience and empower you to navigate the path ahead with grace and resilience.

If you haven't already, imagine receiving news that a loved one has been diagnosed with dementia. The words hang heavy in the air, casting a shadow over the familiar landscape of your life. The person you've known and cherished, who has always been a constant presence, is now facing an uncertain future. Fear, sadness, anger, and confusion may swirl within you, threatening to consume you whole.

In these early moments, it's natural to feel overwhelmed by the magnitude of the diagnosis. You might find yourself grappling with questions like: "How will I cope?" "What will the future hold?" "Will I be able to provide the care my loved one needs?"

While valid and important, these questions can also be paralyzing, hindering your ability to move forward.

This is where acceptance comes in. Acceptance doesn't mean giving up or resigning yourself to a life of despair. It's not about denying the diagnosis's reality or pretending everything is fine. Instead, it's about acknowledging the truth, embracing the challenges, and finding the strength to move forward with courage and compassion. It's about shifting your focus from what was to what is and finding ways to create meaningful experiences in the present moment.

The first step towards acceptance is allowing yourself to feel the full spectrum of emotions that accompany a dementia diagnosis. Grief, anger, fear, sadness, and guilt are all natural responses. It's okay to feel overwhelmed, cry, and express your frustrations. It's vital to permit yourself to experience these emotions, to acknowledge their validity, and to find healthy ways to express them. Whether through journaling, talking to a trusted friend or therapist, or simply allowing yourself to grieve, processing these emotions is an essential part of the healing process.

Denial is a common coping mechanism in the face of a difficult diagnosis. It can manifest as a refusal to believe the diagnosis, minimizing the severity of the symptoms, or avoiding conversations about the future. While denial can offer temporary relief, it ultimately hinders acceptance and prevents you from taking proactive steps to manage the disease and plan for the future.

Overcoming denial requires honesty, self-compassion, and a willingness to face the reality of the situation. It's about acknowledging the changes in your loved one, recognizing the challenges ahead, and accepting the limitations of your abilities as a caregiver. This doesn't mean giving up hope or succumbing to despair. It means embracing the present moment, focusing on what you can control, and finding strength in the face of adversity.

Choosing the right professional for diagnosis and interpretation is crucial. A neurologist specializing in dementia can provide a comprehensive evaluation, explain the diagnosis in clear terms, and answer your questions. They can also offer guidance on treatment options, support services, and strategies for managing the disease. Feel free to seek a second opinion if you have any doubts or concerns.

Communicating the diagnosis to family and friends can be challenging, but it's essential to building a support network. Be honest and open about your loved one's condition; don't be afraid to ask for help. Sharing the burden with others can alleviate stress and create a sense of community. Remember, you're not alone in this journey.

Amidst the challenges, it's important to find hope and positivity. Focus on the strengths and abilities that your loved one still possesses, celebrate the moments of connection and joy, and create new memories together. Remember that even with dementia, life can still be meaningful and fulfilling.

Acceptance is not a one-time event but an ongoing process. It's about learning to adapt to the changes, finding new ways to connect, and cherishing every precious moment. By embracing the journey with courage and compassion, you can empower yourself and your loved one to live life to the fullest, even in the face of dementia.

MANAGING THE GRIEF AND LOSS AFTER A DEMENTIA DIAGNOSIS

A dementia diagnosis is not just a medical label; it's a profound loss that reverberates through the hearts and lives of everyone involved. It's the loss of the person you once knew, the loss of shared memories, the loss of future dreams. It's a grief that can be as deep and complex as any other, and it deserves to be acknowledged, honored, and navigated with compassion.

Grief is a natural and inevitable response to a dementia diagnosis. It's a testament to your love for your loved one, the depth of your connection, and the profound impact this disease has on your lives. You might grieve the loss of their cognitive abilities, independence, personality, or even the future you envisioned together. This overwhelming grief can leave you feeling lost, empty, and adrift in a sea of uncertainty.

It's important to understand that grief doesn't follow a linear path. It's not a series of stages that you neatly progress through, but rather a fluid and unpredictable experience. You might feel waves of sadness one day, anger the next, and moments of acceptance or even gratitude. These emotions are all valid and part of the natural process of healing.

One of the most challenging aspects of grieving a loved one with dementia is the ambiguity of the loss. Unlike other forms of grief, where there's a clear endpoint, dementia is a slow and gradual decline. You might find yourself mourning the loss of your loved one's abilities and personality long before they physically pass away. This can lead to a sense of anticipatory grief, where you're constantly grieving the losses that have already occurred and those that are yet to come.

It's also common to experience a sense of disenfranchised grief, where your feelings of loss are not fully acknowledged or validated by others. Society often views dementia as a natural part of aging, minimizing the profound impact it has on individuals and their families. This can leave caregivers feeling isolated and misunderstood, adding another layer of complexity to their grief.

Navigating this grief requires patience, self-compassion, and a willingness to seek support. There's no right or wrong way to grieve, and what works for one person may not work for another. However, some strategies can help you cope with the emotional challenges and find moments of peace and solace.

One of the most important things is to allow yourself to feel your emotions without judgment. Don't try to suppress your grief or pretend that everything is okay. Instead, acknowledge your feelings, express them in healthy ways, and give yourself time to heal.

Connecting with others who understand what you're going through can be incredibly helpful. Consider joining a support group for dementia caregivers, where you can share your experiences, receive validation, and learn from others who are navigating a similar journey. Talking to a therapist or counselor can also provide a safe space to process your grief and develop coping mechanisms.

Finding ways to honor your loved one's life and legacy can also be a source of comfort. Create a memory book or scrapbook filled with photos and stories. Share their favorite music or movies. Continue traditions that were important to them. These acts of remembrance can help you stay connected to your loved one, even as their memories fade.

Remember, grief is not a sign of weakness; it's a testament to the depth of your love. By acknowledging your grief, seeking support, and finding ways to honor your loved one, you can navigate this challenging journey with grace and resilience.

THE ROLE OF DENIAL IN DEMENTIA AND OVERCOMING IT

When the diagnosis was confirmed as "dementia," a chasm seemed to open beneath my feet. It was as if the world had tilted on its axis, and I didn't want to believe it. The diagnosis felt like a heavy shroud, casting a shadow over my mother's once-vibrant life and plunging all of us into a place of uncertainty and fear. In that moment, denial became my refuge, a protective shield against the harsh reality that threatened to shatter my world.

Denial, in the face of a dementia diagnosis, is not a sign of weakness or a lack of love. It's a natural human response to a devastating blow, a way to cope with the overwhelming emotions that surge forth. It's like a thick fog that descends, blurring the edges of reality and offering a reprieve from the pain.

In those early days, I clung to denial like a lifeline. I convinced myself that the doctor was wrong, that the memory lapses were just a normal part of aging, and that my mother would soon return to her old self. I avoided conversations about the future, focusing instead on the present moment, desperately trying to preserve the illusion of normalcy.

But as time passed, denial became an increasingly heavy burden. The cracks in the facade grew wider, and the truth became harder to ignore. My mother's forgetfulness deepened, her confusion intensified, and her once-familiar world began to crumble around her. I found myself struggling to keep up with the changes, constantly adjusting my expectations and grieving the loss of the woman she once was.

Denial, while initially comforting, can become a formidable obstacle on the path to acceptance. It prevents us from fully acknowledging the reality of the situation, hindering our ability to make informed decisions and provide the best possible care. It can also lead to feelings of isolation and guilt as we grapple with the internal conflict between what we want to believe and what we know to be true.

Overcoming denial is a gradual process, often marked by setbacks and moments of relapse. It requires courage, honesty, and a willingness to confront our deepest fears. It's about acknowledging the pain, embracing the uncertainty, and finding the strength to move forward.

One of the first steps in overcoming denial is education. By learning about dementia, its various forms, its symptoms, and its progression, we can begin to understand the changes we're witnessing in our loved ones. Knowledge is power and can help us dispel the myths and misconceptions that often fuel denial.

Another crucial step is connecting with others who are facing similar challenges. Support groups, online forums, and even casual conversations with other caregivers can provide a sense of community and validation. Hearing the stories of others who have walked this path before us can help us feel less alone and more empowered to face the journey ahead.

It's also important to be kind to ourselves. Caregiving is a demanding and emotionally draining role; sometimes, feeling overwhelmed or discouraged is okay. Permit yourself to grieve, to express your feelings, and to seek help when you need it. Remember, you're not superhuman, and asking for support is okay.

Finally, focus on the present moment. Dementia can rob us of the past and the future, but it can't take away the present. Cherish your time with your loved one, create new memories, and find joy in the simple things. Even amid darkness, there is always light to be seen.

Overcoming denial is not a linear process. There will be good days and bad days, moments of clarity and confusion. But by embracing the journey with courage, compassion, and an open heart, you can find meaning and purpose in the face of adversity. Acceptance is not about giving up; it's about empowering yourself to provide the best possible care for your loved one and to live a life filled with love, even as the world around you changes.

CHOOSING THE RIGHT PROFESSIONAL FOR DIAGNOSIS: NAVIGATING THE MEDICAL MAZE

When faced with the possibility of dementia, the first step is often the most crucial: seeking a diagnosis. But this step can feel like navigating a complex maze filled with unfamiliar terms, confusing options, and a sense of urgency that can be overwhelming. Choosing the proper professional to guide you through this process is essential for accurate diagnosis and receiving the support and guidance you need to embark on this challenging journey.

The first question that often arises is: who should I see? The answer depends on several factors, including your loved one's symptoms, medical history, and your own personal preferences. However, there are a few key professionals who specialize in dementia diagnosis and care.

- <u>Primary Care Physician (PCP)</u>: Your loved one's PCP is often the first point of contact when concerns about cognitive decline arise. They can perform initial screenings, assess overall health, and refer you to specialists if needed. While PCPs may have some experience with dementia, their expertise may be limited compared to specialists.

- <u>Geriatrician</u>: A geriatrician is a physician who specializes in caring for older adults. They have extensive knowledge about age-related health conditions, including dementia, and can provide a comprehensive assessment and recommendations for care.
- <u>Neurologist</u>: A neurologist specializes in brain and nervous system disorders, including dementia. They have the expertise to perform detailed neurological examinations, interpret brain imaging scans, and differentiate between different types of dementia.
- <u>Psychiatrist</u>: A psychiatrist specializes in mental health conditions, including those that can mimic or coexist with dementia, such as depression or anxiety. They can conduct thorough psychiatric evaluations and prescribe medications if necessary.
- <u>Neuropsychologist</u>: A neuropsychologist is a psychologist with specialized training in assessing brain function. They can administer comprehensive cognitive tests to evaluate memory, attention, language, and other cognitive domains. Their insights can be invaluable in diagnosing dementia and identifying specific areas of impairment.

Once you've identified potential professionals, it's essential to do your research and choose someone who is a good fit for you and your loved one. Consider factors such as their experience with dementia, communication style, availability, and willingness to involve you in the decision-making process.

Here are some tips for choosing the right professional:

- <u>Ask for recommendations</u>: Talk to your PCP, friends, family members, or support groups for recommendations of qualified professionals in your area.

- <u>Check credentials</u>: Make sure the professional is licensed and board-certified in their specialty.
- <u>Read online reviews</u>: Look for online reviews and ratings from other patients or caregivers.
- <u>Schedule a consultation</u>: Many professionals offer initial consultations to discuss your concerns and answer questions. This can be an excellent opportunity to gauge their expertise and communication style.
- <u>Trust your instincts</u>: If you are uncomfortable with a particular professional, don't hesitate to seek a second opinion.

Once you've chosen a professional, you must be prepared for your appointment. Bring any relevant medical records, a list of medications your loved one is taking, and a list of questions or concerns you want to address. Be honest and open about your observations and any changes you've noticed in your loved one's behavior or cognitive abilities.

Remember, the diagnostic process is a collaborative effort. You are your loved one's advocate; your insights and observations are valuable. Feel free to ask questions, seek clarification, and express your concerns. The right professional will listen to you, respect your input, and work with you to develop a personalized care plan.

Choosing the right professional for diagnosis is a critical step in navigating the dementia journey (Alzheimer's Association, 2024). It's about finding a trusted guide who can help you understand the complexities of the disease, provide accurate information, and offer compassionate support. By making an informed choice, you can empower yourself and your loved one to face the challenges ahead with knowledge, confidence, and hope.

INTERPRETING THE DIAGNOSIS WITH A NEUROLOGIST: DECODING THE MEDICAL JARGON

The appointment with the neurologist can feel like a pivotal moment, a crossroads where anticipation and anxiety intertwine. You've gathered your loved one's medical records, prepared a list of questions, and steeled yourself for the possibility of a dementia diagnosis. Sitting in the sterile examination room, surrounded by medical charts and unfamiliar equipment, you may feel vulnerable, hoping for clarity but fearing the unknown.

The neurologist, with their years of training and expertise, holds the key to unlocking the mystery of your loved one's cognitive decline. Their words carry weight; their explanations can either relieve or deepen your concerns. It's essential to approach this interaction as a partnership, actively participating in the conversation and seeking to understand the intricacies of the diagnosis.

The neurologist will likely begin by reviewing your loved one's medical history, asking about their symptoms, and conducting a thorough neurological examination. This may involve tests of reflexes, coordination, balance, and sensory function. They may also order additional tests, such as blood work or brain imaging scans, to rule out other potential causes of cognitive impairment and to gain a clearer picture of the brain's structure and function.

Once all the information is gathered, the neurologist will discuss their findings and provide a diagnosis. This is often the moment of truth when the fog of uncertainty begins to lift, and the reality of the situation comes into focus. The neurologist may use medical jargon and complex terminology, so feel free to ask for clarification if you need help understanding something.

It's also important to remember that a dementia diagnosis is not a one-size-fits-all label. There are different types of dementia, each with its unique symptoms and progression patterns. The neurologist will explain the specific type of dementia your loved one has been diagnosed with, as well as its likely cause and expected course. They will also discuss available treatment options, potential side effects, and the importance of ongoing monitoring and care.

As you listen to the neurologist's explanations, it's natural to feel a range of emotions. You might feel relief that there's finally an answer, sadness at the confirmation of your fears, or even anger at the unfairness of the situation. It's important to acknowledge these emotions and allow yourself to process them.

Don't be afraid to ask questions. This is your opportunity to better understand your loved one's condition and participate actively in their care. Thankfully, the Alzheimer's Association (2023) provides a helpful resource, 'Questions for Your Doctor,' which offers guidance on what to ask your healthcare provider to gain a deeper understanding of the diagnosis, treatment options, and available support. Some questions you might want to ask include:

- What type of dementia has my loved one been diagnosed with?
- What is the likely cause of their dementia?
- What are the expected symptoms and progression of the disease?
- What treatment options are available, and what are their potential benefits and side effects?

- What lifestyle modifications can we make to support my loved one's cognitive health?
- What resources and support services are available to us?

The neurologist should be able to provide clear and concise answers to your questions, using language that you can understand. If you feel overwhelmed or confused, feel free to ask for clarification or to have them repeat information.

Remember, you are your loved one's advocate. Your role is to ensure that they receive the best possible care and support. By actively participating in the diagnostic process and seeking to understand the intricacies of the diagnosis, you can empower yourself to make informed decisions and navigate the journey ahead with confidence and compassion.

Interpreting the diagnosis with a neurologist is not just about receiving a label; it's about gaining knowledge, understanding the implications, and forging a partnership with a healthcare professional who can guide you through the complexities of dementia care. It's about finding clarity amid uncertainty and hope in the face of adversity.

COMMUNICATING THE DIAGNOSIS: TALKING TO FAMILY AND FRIENDS

Sharing a dementia diagnosis with family and friends can be a delicate and emotionally charged process. It's a moment of vulnerability, where you reveal a deeply personal struggle and invite others into a world of uncertainty and change. However, communicating the diagnosis is also an essential step in building a support network, fostering understanding, and ensuring that your loved one receives the care and compassion they deserve. The Alzheimer's Society (2023) offers valuable advice on how to approach these conversations, emphasizing the importance of honesty, openness, and allowing loved ones to express their own emotions.

The first step is deciding who to tell and when. It's natural to want to protect your loved one's privacy but keeping the diagnosis a secret can create unnecessary stress and isolation. Consider starting with close family members and trusted friends, gradually expanding the circle as you feel comfortable.

When sharing the news, choose a time and place where you can have an open and honest conversation without distractions. Be prepared for a range of reactions, from shock and sadness to disbelief and denial. It's essential to allow others to express their emotions and validate their feelings. Remember, everyone processes information differently, and it may take time for some people to grasp the implications of the diagnosis entirely.

Be clear and direct when communicating the diagnosis. Avoid using euphemisms or sugarcoating the truth. Explain the type of dementia your loved one has been diagnosed with, its potential impact on their cognitive abilities, and the expected course of the disease. Provide information about available resources and support services and emphasize the importance of early intervention and ongoing care.

It's also important to address any concerns or questions that family and friends may have. They might be worried about how to interact with their loved one, how to offer support, or what the future holds. Be patient and understanding. Offer reassurance that you're all in this together.

Remember, communication is a two-way street. Encourage family and friends to share their feelings and concerns openly. Listen actively, validate their emotions, and offer support. This open dialogue can foster understanding, strengthen relationships, and create a shared responsibility in caring for your loved one.

As you communicate the diagnosis, emphasize the importance of focusing on the present moment and celebrating the personhood of your loved one. Remind others that dementia doesn't define them and that they still have the capacity for joy, love, and connection. Encourage family and friends to visit, engage in activities, and create meaningful experiences with your loved one.

Feel free to ask for help. Caregiving can be a demanding and isolating experience, and it's okay to lean on others for support. Whether it's help with household chores, running errands, or simply providing a listening ear, don't hesitate to reach out to your network.

Finally, remember that communication is an ongoing process. As your loved one's condition changes, you may need to have additional conversations with family and friends. Keep them updated on any new developments, challenges, or successes. By maintaining open lines of communication, you can ensure that everyone feels informed, supported, and connected throughout the journey.

Sharing a dementia diagnosis is not easy, but it's a crucial step in building a solid support network and ensuring that your loved one receives the care and compassion they deserve. Communicating openly and honestly fosters understanding, strengthens relationships, and creates a community of love and support that will sustain you through the challenges ahead.

FINDING HOPE AND POSITIVITY AMIDST THE DIAGNOSIS

In the face of a dementia diagnosis, the world can seem bleak and unforgiving. The weight of the unknown, the fear of what lies ahead, and the grief of losing the person you once knew can cast a long shadow over your life. It's easy to succumb to despair, to feel like there's no light at the end of the tunnel. But even in the darkest times, hope and positivity can blossom, offering a glimmer of light and a path toward resilience.

Finding hope and positivity amidst a dementia diagnosis is not about denying the challenges or pretending that everything is fine. It's about acknowledging the difficulties while also recognizing the opportunities for growth, connection, and even joy. It's about shifting your perspective, focusing on what you can control, and finding meaning in the present moment. It's about recognizing that even though dementia may change the landscape of your relationship with your loved one, it doesn't extinguish the love and connection you share.

One way to cultivate hope is to educate yourself about dementia. Knowledge is power, and the more you understand the disease, the less frightening it becomes. Learn about the different stages, the available treatments, and the support services to help you navigate the journey. Connect with other caregivers, read books and articles, and attend workshops or seminars. By arming yourself with information, you can feel more empowered and less overwhelmed. Understanding the science behind dementia can help you anticipate changes and make informed care decisions. It can also dispel misconceptions and reduce the stigma associated with the disease.

Another crucial aspect of fostering hope is embracing the power of community. Seek support groups, both online and in person, where you can connect with other caregivers facing similar challenges. Sharing your experiences, listening to others, and receiving validation can be incredibly empowering and uplifting. It reminds you that you're not alone in this journey and that there are people who understand what you're going through. These connections can offer a lifeline, providing emotional support, practical advice, and a sense of belonging.

It's also important to celebrate the small victories. Whether it's a successful trip to the grocery store, a shared laugh over a silly joke, or a moment of clarity and recognition, these small wins can provide a much-needed boost of positivity. Don't underestimate the power of these seemingly insignificant moments; they can be a source of immense joy and a reminder of the enduring bond you share with your loved one. Each smile, each shared memory, each moment of connection, no matter how fleeting, is a treasure to be cherished. In the challenges, these moments of joy remind us of the beauty and resilience of the human spirit.

Humor can also be a powerful tool in navigating the dementia journey. While there will undoubtedly be challenging moments, finding ways to laugh and share lighthearted moments can provide a much-needed respite. It can also help to diffuse tension, reduce stress, and strengthen your connection with your loved one. Laughter truly is medicine, and it can bring a sense of lightness and joy even in adversity. Sharing a silly joke, watching a funny movie, or simply reminiscing about happy memories can create moments of shared laughter that transcend the challenges of dementia.

Finally, and perhaps most importantly, remember to take care of yourself. Caregiving can be physically and emotionally draining, and it's essential to prioritize your own well-being. Make time for activities you enjoy, connect with friends and family, and seek professional help if needed. By taking care of yourself, you'll be better equipped to care for your loved one and to maintain a positive outlook. Remember, you can't pour from an empty cup. Taking breaks, engaging in hobbies, and nurturing your own physical and emotional health are not selfish acts; they are essential for sustainable and compassionate caregiving.

Finding hope and positivity amidst a dementia diagnosis is not always easy, but it's essential for both your well-being and the well-being of your loved one. By focusing on the present moment, celebrating small victories, finding humor during challenges, connecting with others, and prioritizing self-care, you can create a more positive and empowering experience for everyone involved. Remember, even in the face of darkness, there is always light to be found. And as you walk this path, may you find strength in the love you share, resilience in the face of adversity, and hope in the enduring power of the human spirit.

There is no greater act of love than caring for someone who once cared for you. – Unknown

DAILY CARE AND MANAGING BEHAVIORAL CHANGES

When your loved one is diagnosed with dementia, your home transforms from a familiar haven into a place of confusion and risk. Simple tasks like finding the bathroom or remembering how to use the stove can become monumental challenges. As a caregiver, one of the most impactful things you can do is to adapt your living space to create a dementia-friendly environment. Here, your loved one can feel safe, secure, and supported, even as their cognitive abilities decline.

The first step in creating a dementia-friendly home is decluttering and simplifying. Imagine walking into a room filled with knick-knacks, piles of papers, and furniture blocking pathways. For someone with dementia, this visual clutter can be overwhelming and disorienting. Removing unnecessary items and organizing belongings clearly and logically can reduce confusion and create a more peaceful atmosphere.

Consider labeling drawers and cupboards with clear, easy-to-read labels or even pictures. This simple step can make a world of difference, empowering your loved one to maintain a sense of independence and reducing frustration when searching for everyday items. Keeping frequently used items within easy reach is also essential, minimizing the need for rummaging or searching through cluttered spaces.

Lighting plays a crucial role in creating a safe and comfortable environment. Ensure that all areas of the house are well lit, especially hallways, stairways, and bathrooms. Adequate lighting can prevent falls and reduce disorientation, particularly during nighttime awakenings. Use nightlights strategically to provide a gentle glow and guide your loved one safely through the house. Be mindful of glare and shadows, which can create visual distortions and contribute to confusion. Opt for soft, natural lighting whenever possible.

Safety is paramount in a dementia-friendly home. Install handrails on stairways and in bathrooms to provide support and stability. Consider adding grab bars near toilets and showers to prevent falls. Remove throw rugs or other tripping hazards, and secure loose cords or wires that could pose a risk. Install safety locks on doors and windows to prevent wandering, and consider using a monitoring system or alarms to keep track of your loved one's movements and ensure their safety.

Creating a calm and soothing environment is also essential. Use soft, calming colors on walls and furniture, avoiding busy patterns or excessive decorations that can be visually overwhelming. Play familiar music or nature sounds to create a peaceful atmosphere and reduce agitation. Provide comfortable seating areas with good lighting for reading or conversation, encouraging relaxation and engagement.

The bedroom should be a haven of tranquility and rest. Keep the room uncluttered and well-ventilated, ensuring a comfortable temperature. Make sure the bed is easy to get in and out of and consider using adaptive bedding or assistive devices if needed. Use blackout curtains or blinds to promote restful sleep, especially if your loved one experiences sundowning or nighttime confusion. A familiar and calming environment can significantly improve sleep quality and reduce anxiety.

The bathroom can be a particularly challenging area for individuals with dementia. Install grab bars and non-slip mats in the shower or tub to prevent falls. Use a shower chair or bench for added support and opt for a handheld showerhead for easier bathing. Ensure the toilet is easily accessible and well-lit, and consider installing a raised toilet seat or grab bars for added safety. Use contrasting colors for towels, toilet seats, and floors to enhance visibility and reduce confusion.

In the kitchen, simplify meal preparation and reduce the risk of accidents. Remove any sharp objects or appliances that could be dangerous. Use clear containers for food storage and label them with pictures or simple words to aid recognition. Consider using unbreakable dishes and utensils to prevent injuries. Keep the kitchen clean and organized, minimizing clutter and distractions.

Remember, creating a dementia-friendly home is an ongoing process. As your loved one's needs and abilities evolve, be prepared to adjust and modify along the way. Observe their behaviors, listen to their cues, and adapt your home environment to support their changing needs. Creating a safe, comfortable, and supportive space can enhance their quality of life, reduce anxiety, and foster a sense of dignity and belonging. Your home can become a haven where love, compassion, and understanding prevail, even in the face of dementia's challenges. The Alzheimer's Society (2023) offers a comprehensive guide on 'Making your home dementia-friendly,' with practical advice on everything from decluttering and improving lighting to installing safety features and creating a calming environment

DAILY ROUTINES FOR DEMENTIA CARE: STRUCTURE AND FLEXIBILITY

In the world of dementia care, the delicate dance between structure and flexibility is critical to creating a sense of normalcy and reducing anxiety for your loved one. Establishing consistent routines can provide a sense of predictability and security while allowing flexibility to accommodate their changing needs and moods. It's a balancing act that requires patience, observation, and a willingness to adapt.

Start by identifying your loved one's natural rhythms and preferences. When do they typically wake up, eat, and go to bed? What activities do they enjoy, and when do they seem most engaged? Use this information to create a daily schedule that aligns with their natural patterns, providing a sense of familiarity and comfort.

A consistent routine can help reduce confusion and agitation, particularly for individuals in the later stages of dementia. Knowing what to expect can provide a sense of control and reduce anxiety, promoting a calmer and more peaceful environment. However, it's important to remember that flexibility is also crucial. Dementia can cause unpredictable mood swings, fatigue, and changes in behavior. Be prepared to adjust the schedule as needed, allowing for rest periods, spontaneous activities, and moments of quiet reflection.

Mealtimes can be a source of both nourishment and connection. Establish regular mealtimes and create a pleasant dining atmosphere. Offer familiar foods that your loved one enjoys, and be mindful of any dietary restrictions or swallowing difficulties. Please encourage them to participate in meal preparation or setting the table, as these activities can foster a sense of purpose and engagement.

Personal care routines, such as bathing, dressing, and grooming, can become challenging as dementia progresses. Approach these tasks with patience, respect, and a focus on preserving your loved one's dignity. Please choose a time of day when they are most relaxed and receptive and offer choices whenever possible. Use gentle touch and soothing words and be mindful of any physical limitations or sensitivities.

Activities and exercise are also essential components of a daily routine. Engage your loved one in activities they enjoy, such as listening to music, looking at photos, or going for walks. Encourage physical activity, even if it's just gentle stretching or walking around the house. Exercise can improve mood, sleep, and overall well-being.

Sundowning, a phenomenon characterized by increased confusion and agitation in the late afternoon and evening, is a common challenge in dementia care (Canevelli et al., 2016). As the day progresses, be mindful of the potential for sundowning, where agitation and confusion increase in the late afternoon or evening. Create a calm and relaxing evening routine, avoiding stimulating activities or loud noises. Offer a light snack or warm beverage and encourage relaxation techniques like deep breathing or listening to calming music.

Observe your loved one's cues throughout the day and adjust the routine as needed. If they seem tired, offer a rest period. If they're agitated, try a calming activity or a change of scenery. If they're particularly engaged in an activity, allow them to continue for as long as they enjoy it.

Remember, the goal is to create a routine that provides structure and predictability while allowing for flexibility and spontaneity. Finding the right balance can make a supportive and nurturing environment that promotes your loved one's well-being and enhances their quality of life.

NAVIGATING PERSONALITY AND BEHAVIORAL
CHANGES: THE SHIFTING TIDES OF DEMENTIA

One of the most heart-wrenching aspects of dementia is witnessing the gradual transformation of your loved one's personality and behavior. The once familiar person, with their unique quirks, passions, and sense of humor, may slowly fade away, replaced by someone who seems distant, unpredictable, or even unrecognizable. This transformation can be a source of profound grief and confusion for caregivers, leaving them feeling lost and adrift in a sea of change.

It's important to remember that these changes are not intentional or malicious. They directly result from the damage dementia inflicts on the brain, affecting areas responsible for personality, emotions, and behavior. As the disease progresses, the delicate balance of neurotransmitters and neural pathways is disrupted, leading to a range of behavioral and personality shifts.

As Lyketsos et al. (2011) explain, these neuropsychiatric symptoms, such as agitation, anxiety, and even aggression, are common in Alzheimer's disease and other forms of dementia. Understanding the underlying causes of these behaviors and learning effective strategies for managing them became essential in providing compassionate care. Your loved one may become easily frustrated, restless, or even verbally or physically aggressive. They might experience paranoia, delusions, or hallucinations, leading to further distress and confusion. These behaviors can be triggered by a variety of factors, including changes in routine, unfamiliar environments, or even sensory overload. It's essential to approach these situations with empathy and understanding, recognizing that your loved one is not acting out of malice but rather responding to the challenges they're facing.

Another common change is apathy or withdrawal. Your loved one may lose interest in activities they once enjoyed, become less communicative, or seem emotionally flat. This withdrawal can be a coping mechanism for dealing with the overwhelming cognitive changes they're experiencing. It's important to remember that this apathy does not reflect their love for you or their desire to connect, but rather a symptom of the disease. While it can be disheartening, it's crucial to maintain a consistent presence and offer opportunities for engagement, even if they are initially declined.

Changes in sleep patterns are also common in dementia. Individuals may experience insomnia, frequent nighttime awakenings, or daytime drowsiness. These sleep disturbances can further exacerbate cognitive impairment and contribute to agitation and confusion. Establishing a consistent bedtime routine, creating a calming sleep environment, and limiting daytime naps can help regulate sleep patterns. It's also important to address any underlying medical conditions that may contribute to sleep problems.

As a caregiver, navigating these personality and behavioral changes requires patience, understanding, and a willingness to adapt. It's essential to remember that your loved one is not acting out of spite or malice, but rather responding to the challenges they're facing. You can create a more supportive and less stressful environment by approaching these situations with empathy and compassion.

One helpful skill to develop is learning to identify triggers for agitation or anxiety. Is there a particular time of day when your loved one becomes more restless? Are there certain activities or environments that seem to provoke distress? I learned, as Moniz-Cook, Vernooij-Dassen, and Woods (2006) emphasize in their research, that identifying and understanding these triggers is crucial for managing challenging behaviors and creating a more peaceful environment for both the person with dementia and their caregiver. Once you identify these triggers, you can take steps to avoid them or modify them to create a more calming experience. For example, if your loved one becomes agitated during bath time, try offering a sponge bath or a shower chair instead.

Maintaining a consistent routine is important, as predictability can provide a sense of security and reduce anxiety. However, be flexible and allow for spontaneity when needed. If your loved one is resisting a particular activity, don't force it. Instead, offer alternatives that will enable them to rest and recharge. Remember, the goal is to create a supportive and nurturing environment that promotes your loved one's well-being and dignity.

Communication is key, even when it becomes challenging. Use simple, straightforward language, and avoid overwhelming your loved one with too much information at once. Be patient, allow them time to process your words, and validate their feelings. Even if they can't express themselves verbally, they can still understand your tone of voice and body language. Non-verbal communication, such as touch, facial expressions, and gestures, can be powerful tools for connecting and conveying your love and support.

Remember, you're not alone in this journey. Seek support from other caregivers, healthcare professionals, and community resources. Don't be afraid to ask for help when you need it. By taking care of yourself, you'll be better equipped to care for your loved one and to navigate the challenges of dementia. Remember, self-care is not selfish; it's essential for your own well-being and for the well-being of those you care for.

Navigating personality and behavioral changes is undoubtedly one of the most challenging aspects of dementia caregiving. It requires a deep source of empathy, patience, and resilience. But by understanding the underlying causes, implementing effective strategies, and seeking support, you can create a more peaceful and harmonious environment for both you and your loved one. Remember, your love and presence are the greatest gifts you can offer, and they can transform even the most difficult moments into opportunities for connection and growth.

COMMUNICATION TECHNIQUES FOR EVERY STAGE OF DEMENTIA

Communication, the cornerstone of human interaction, connects us to the world and those we hold dear. When dementia enters the picture, this bridge can become fragile, its foundations weakened by the relentless erosion of cognitive abilities. As caregivers, we find ourselves navigating uncharted waters, searching for new ways to connect, understand, and express love in the face of a disease that threatens to steal away the very essence of our loved ones.

Effective communication in dementia care is not just about words; it's about creating a safe and supportive space where your loved one feels heard, understood, and valued. It's about recognizing their emotions, honoring their dignity, and fostering a sense of connection, even in the face of communication challenges. It requires patience, empathy, and a willingness to adapt your communication style to meet their changing needs. It's a delicate balance where listening, observing, and responding with compassion are paramount. The Alzheimer's Society (2023) offers valuable insights into how communication changes throughout the different stages of the disease.

In the early stages of dementia, communication may still be relatively easy, although you might notice subtle changes. Your loved one may have difficulty finding the right words, following complex conversations, or remembering recent events. These initial stumbles can be frustrating, but they also offer an opportunity to practice patience and understanding. Speak slowly and clearly, using simple, direct language. Avoid distractions and maintain eye contact, showing your loved one you are fully present and engaged in the conversation.

As dementia progresses, communication becomes more challenging. Your loved one may have difficulty understanding your words, expressing their thoughts clearly, or even recognizing familiar faces. In these moments, it's crucial to rely on non-verbal communication, the language of the heart. A warm smile, a gentle touch, or a reassuring hug can convey love and support even when words fail. Sitting close, holding their hand, or offering a comforting presence can speak volumes, reminding them that they are not alone.

Remember, communication is a two-way street. Even if your loved one's verbal abilities are limited, they can still understand your tone of voice and body language. Speak calmly and reassuringly, avoid raising your voice or becoming frustrated, and pay attention to their non-verbal cues. Are they fidgeting, looking away, or becoming agitated? These cues can provide valuable insights into their emotional state and help you adjust your communication accordingly. Be attuned to their needs, even if they are unspoken.

Validation is another critical component of effective communication in dementia care. It's about acknowledging your loved one's feelings and experiences, even if they seem illogical or confusing. Avoid arguing or correcting them, which can lead to frustration and agitation. Instead, try to enter their reality, understand their perspective, and respond with empathy and compassion. For example, if your loved one insists they must go home, even though they are already home, don't contradict them. Instead, try to redirect their attention or offer reassurance that they are safe and loved.

Validation is about honoring their reality, even if it differs from yours.

In the later stages of dementia, communication may become primarily non-verbal. Your loved one may have difficulty understanding spoken language, but they can still respond to touch, music, and familiar faces. Spend time being present with them, holding their hand, singing their favorite songs, or looking at photos together. These moments of connection, even without words, can be incredibly meaningful and comforting. They remind us that love transcends language and that even in the face of profound cognitive decline, the human spirit remains capable of deep and meaningful connection.

Remember, communication is not just about conveying information; it's about fostering connection, expressing love, and preserving dignity. Even when words become elusive, there are countless ways to communicate with your loved one. By being patient, empathetic, and adaptable, you can create a space where they feel heard, understood, and valued, even as they navigate the challenges of dementia. Your presence, your touch, and your unwavering love can speak volumes, creating a bridge of connection that transcends the limitations of language. In these quiet moments of shared humanity, you may discover a depth of love and understanding that surpasses anything you've ever known.

MANAGING SUNDOWNING: STRATEGIES FOR LATE-DAY CONFUSION

As the sun begins its descent, casting long shadows and painting the sky in hues of orange and gold, a familiar restlessness may settle upon your loved one with dementia. This phenomenon, known as sundowning, is a common challenge for caregivers, marked by increased confusion, agitation, and anxiety as the day draws to a close. It's a time of heightened vulnerability when the familiar world becomes disorienting, and shadows transform into frightening figures.

Sundowning can manifest in various ways, from pacing and restlessness to irritability, anger, or even paranoia. It can disrupt sleep patterns, create safety concerns, and leave both the individual and their caregivers feeling exhausted and over-whelmed. While the exact causes of sundowning remain a mystery, researchers believe it may be linked to disruptions in the body's internal clock, changes in light exposure, fatigue, or even underlying medical conditions.

As a caregiver, dealing with sundowning requires patience, understanding, and strategies to create a calm and reassuring environment. It's about anticipating the challenges, recognizing the triggers, and responding with compassion and flexibility.

One of the most effective strategies is to establish a consistent evening routine. Predictability can be a powerful antidote to confusion and anxiety. Start winding down early in the evening, avoiding stimulating activities or loud noises. Dim the lights, play calming music, and create a peaceful, relaxing atmosphere. Offer a light snack or warm beverage and encourage your loved one to engage in calming activities, such as reading, listening to music, or taking a warm bath.

Light therapy can also be beneficial in regulating sleep-wake cycles and reducing sundowning symptoms. Expose your loved one to bright light during the day, especially in the morning, and limit their exposure to artificial light in the evening. This can help reset their internal clock and promote more restful sleep. Research by Riemersma-van der Lek et al. (2008) suggests that bright light therapy can be an effective intervention for improving sleep and reducing sundowning behaviors in indi-viduals with dementia. It's like resetting the internal clock, promoting a more natural rhythm of daytime alertness and nighttime rest.

Pay attention to your loved one's physical needs. Please ensure they are comfortable, well-hydrated, and have used the bathroom before bedtime. Address any pain or discomfort they may be experiencing, as these can contribute to agitation and restlessness. Consider offering a gentle massage or warm compress to promote relaxation.

Engage in calming activities together. Reading a favorite book, listening to soothing music, or looking at old photographs can create a sense of connection and comfort. Avoid stimulating activities or conversations that might trigger anxiety or confusion. Focus on building a peaceful and reassuring environment where your loved one feels safe and secure.

If your loved one becomes agitated or distressed, remain calm and patient. Avoid arguing or trying to reason with them, as this can escalate the situation. Instead, validate their feelings, offer reassurance, and try to redirect their attention to a calming activity. If necessary, provide a quiet space where they can de-escalate and regain their composure.

Remember, sundowning is a symptom of dementia, not a personal choice. Your loved one is not intentionally trying to be difficult or disruptive. They are simply struggling to cope with the challenges of the disease. By approaching sundowning with empathy and understanding, you can create a more peaceful and supportive environment for both you and your loved one.

If sundowning symptoms persist or become severe, consult with your loved one's doctor. They may recommend medications or other interventions to help manage agitation and promote restful sleep. Don't hesitate to seek professional guidance and support; it's essential to providing compassionate care.

Managing sundowning requires an approach that combines environmental modifications, calming activities, and attentive caregiving. By understanding the triggers, implementing effective strategies, and prioritizing your loved one's comfort and well-being, you can navigate the challenges of late-day confusion with grace and resilience. Remember, you're not alone in this journey. Seek support from other caregivers, healthcare professionals, and community resources. Together, you can create a haven of peace and understanding for your loved one, even as the sun sets on another day.

ACTIVITIES TO ENGAGE AND STIMULATE: NURTURING THE SPARK WITHIN

While dementia may dim the light of memory and cognition, it doesn't extinguish the spark of life that resides within your loved one. Engaging in meaningful activities can ignite that spark, fostering joy, connection, and a sense of purpose. It's about creating opportunities for shared experiences, stimulating the senses, and tapping into the wellspring of remaining memories and emotions. It's about recognizing that even in the face of cognitive decline, there is still a person here with unique likes, dislikes, and preferences.

The key to choosing activities is to focus on what your loved one enjoys and is still capable of doing. Take a walk down memory lane, exploring their past hobbies, interests, and passions. Perhaps they were an avid gardener, a music enthusiast, or a skilled craftsman. Tailor activities to these interests, creating opportunities to reminisce and rekindle those passions.

Remember, abilities and interests may change as dementia progresses, so be flexible and adaptable. What brings joy today may not tomorrow, and that's okay. The goal is to create moments of engagement, stimulation, and connection, however fleeting they may be. It's about being present with your loved one, adapting to their needs, and celebrating the moments of joy that emerge along the way.

Music uniquely can transcend the barriers of dementia, evoking emotions and memories that words alone cannot reach. Create playlists of your loved one's favorite songs, sing along together, or sit and listen to the melodies that once filled their lives with joy. Music can also be a powerful tool for managing agitation and promoting relaxation. Consider playing calming instrumental music or nature sounds during times of restlessness or anxiety. The rhythm and melody can soothe the soul and create a sense of peace.

Reminiscing can be a source of comfort and connection. Look through old photographs, share stories about family and friends, or revisit places that hold special meaning. These trips down memory lane can spark conversations, evoke laughter, and create a sense of shared history. Even if your loved one struggles to recall specific details, the emotions and feelings associated with these memories can still be deeply felt. These shared moments can foster a sense of intimacy and belonging, reminding your loved one of their rich and meaningful life.

Van der Steen et al. (2014) highlight in their research, creative activities can have a profound impact on the quality of life for individuals with dementia. Creative activities can provide a sense of accomplishment and self-expression. Encourage your loved one to paint, draw, write, or engage in other forms of artistic expression. These activities can tap into their creativity, boost self-esteem, and provide a sense of purpose. Don't worry about perfection; the creating process matters most. Creating can be therapeutic, allowing for self-expression and a sense of control, even as other abilities may decline.

Simple games and puzzles can also be enjoyable and stimulating. Choose activities that are appropriate for your loved one's cognitive abilities and be patient if they struggle or become frustrated. The goal is to have fun and create moments of shared laughter and connection. Simple card games, board games, or even sorting objects by color or shape can provide mental stimulation and a sense of accomplishment.

Outdoor activities can be particularly beneficial for individuals with dementia. Spending time in nature can reduce stress, improve mood, and promote physical activity. Take a walk in the park, sit on a bench and enjoy the sunshine, or listen to the birds singing. The sights, sounds, and smells of nature can evoke a sense of peace and tranquility, offering a welcome respite from the confines of indoor living. Even a short stroll in the garden or sitting on the porch can provide a refreshing change of scenery and a connection to the natural world.

As dementia progresses, it's vital to adapt activities to meet your loved one's changing needs. Focus on simple, repetitive tasks that they can still enjoy and find meaningful. Folding laundry, sorting objects, or helping with meal preparation can provide a sense of purpose and accomplishment. Remember, the goal is not to complete the task perfectly but to create an opportunity for engagement and connection. These activities can also help maintain motor skills and provide a sense of routine and familiarity.

In the later stages of dementia, when communication and mobility may be limited, focus on providing sensory stimulation and comfort. Offer a gentle touch, play soothing music, or read aloud from a favorite book. These simple acts of love and kindness can bring immense comfort and peace. Even when words are no longer understood, the warmth of your touch and the sound of your voice can convey love and reassurance.

Remember, engaging in activities with your loved one is not just about keeping them busy; it's about creating opportunities for joy, connection, and a sense of purpose. It's about celebrating their unique personality, honoring their past, and creating new memories in the present moment. By nurturing the spark within, you can help your loved one live a more fulfilling and meaningful life, even in the face of dementia's challenges.

The best way to find yourself is to lose yourself in the service of others." - Mahatma Gandhi

CHAPTER 3 PRACTICAL EXERCISE

Take some time to reflect on your communication style with your loved one. Then, try to answer the following questions in your journal. Do this periodically to see how your opinions have changed:

1. What styles of communication work best for you? Are they visual learners, auditory learners, or maybe most responsive to touch?
2. Have you noticed any change in the way you communicate with them?
3. What are your biggest challenges faced in communicating with them?
4. What communication strategies have you found successful? Share specific examples with others in your support group, family and close friends who help you on occasion.

4

BEYOND MEDICATION: LIFESTYLE, DIET AND WELLNESS

As the saying goes, "You are what you eat," and this holds true even in the face of dementia. The foods we nourish our bodies with profoundly impact overall health, including brain health, cognitive function, and emotional well-being. For individuals with dementia, a well-balanced and nutritious diet is not just a matter of sustenance; it's a vital component of their care plan, potentially influencing symptom management, preserving cognitive abilities, and enhancing their overall quality of life.

Just as a car requires the correct type of fuel to run smoothly, the brain needs a steady supply of specific nutrients to function optimally. Think of the brain as a bustling metropolis, with billions of neurons communicating through intricate networks. These networks rely on a constant flow of energy, building materials, and messengers to maintain their function and resilience. A diet rich in fruits, vegetables, whole grains, lean protein, and healthy fats provides the essential building blocks for brain health, supporting memory, attention, and other cognitive functions. It's like providing the brain with a premium fuel blend that enhances performance and protects it from wear and tear.

One of the most promising dietary approaches for dementia prevention and management is the Mediterranean diet. Research by Lourida et al. (2019) highlights the positive impact of a Mediterranean diet on cognitive function and dementia risk. This heart-healthy eating pattern emphasizes plant-based foods, such as fruits, vegetables, whole grains, legumes, and nuts. It also includes moderate amounts of fish, poultry, and dairy, with limited consumption of red meat and processed foods. Studies have shown that adhering to a Mediterranean diet can reduce the risk of cognitive decline, potentially delaying the onset of dementia or slowing its progression. It's like providing the brain with a diverse and vibrant ecosystem where various nutrients work together to promote optimal health and resilience.

Certain foods and nutrients have explicitly linked to improved cognitive function and brain health. Omega-3 fatty acids in fatty fish such as salmon, tuna, and sardines are essential for brain development and function. They help maintain the structure of brain cell membranes, support communication between neurons, and reduce inflammation. Antioxidants, abundant in berries, dark leafy greens, and other colorful fruits and vegetables, protect brain cells from damage caused by free radicals. These unstable molecules can contribute to oxidative stress and cell death. B vitamins in whole grains, legumes, and leafy greens play a vital role in energy production and neurotransmitter synthesis, ensuring the brain has the fuel it needs to function optimally.

While these specific nutrients have gained attention for their potential brain-boosting benefits, it's important to remember that a holistic approach to nutrition is key. The brain thrives on a diverse and balanced diet that provides many vitamins, minerals, and other essential nutrients. It's not just about incorporating specific "superfoods" but creating a sustainable and enjoyable eating pattern that nourishes the body and mind.

On the other hand, some foods can have a detrimental effect on brain health and may even increase the risk of dementia. Highly processed foods, sugary drinks, and excessive amounts of saturated and trans fats have been linked to cognitive decline and an increased risk of Alzheimer's disease. These foods can contribute to inflammation, oxidative stress, and insulin resistance, all of which can damage brain cells and impair cognitive function. Limiting these foods and prioritizing whole, unprocessed options whenever possible is important.

As a caregiver, navigating the complexities of nutrition and dementia can be challenging. It's important to be mindful of your loved one's changing needs and preferences and any swallowing difficulties or dietary restrictions they may have. Please consult with a registered dietitian or healthcare professional for personalized guidance and recommendations tailored to their specific needs.

Remember, food is not just about nourishment; it's also about pleasure, connection, and cultural identity. Incorporate your loved one's favorite foods and family recipes into their diet, honoring their traditions and preferences. Make mealtimes enjoyable and social, fostering a sense of connection and well-being.

By prioritizing nutrition and making informed dietary choices, you can play an active role in supporting your loved one's brain health and overall well-being. It's a simple yet powerful way to express your love and care, nourishing not just their body but also their spirit.

THE ROLE OF PHYSICAL EXERCISE IN SLOWING COGNITIVE DECLINE

In the intricate dance between body and mind, physical exercise emerges as a powerful partner, capable of influencing not just our physical health but also the resilience of our cognitive abilities. For individuals with dementia, regular physical activity can be a lifeline, offering many benefits that extend far beyond mere fitness. It's about stimulating the brain, fostering a sense of well-being, and slowing cognitive decline.

Imagine the brain as a muscle that requires regular exercise to maintain strength and flexibility. Physical activity increases blood flow to the brain, delivering vital oxygen and nutrients that nourish neurons and promote the growth of new connections. It also stimulates the production of brain-derived neurotrophic factor (BDNF), a protein that acts as fertilizer for the brain, promoting the survival and growth of neurons.

Research has consistently shown that regular exercise can have a profound impact on cognitive function, particularly in individuals with dementia. Studies have demonstrated that physical activity can improve memory, attention, and executive function and reduce the risk of falls and depression. It can also enhance mood, sleep quality, and overall sense of well-being, contributing to a more positive and fulfilling life experience.

The beauty of exercise is its accessibility and versatility. It doesn't have to involve strenuous workouts or expensive gym memberships. Simple activities like walking, gardening, dancing, or even chair exercises can provide significant benefits. The key is finding activities your loved one enjoys and can do safely.

Start by incorporating short bursts of physical activity into their daily routine. A 10-minute walk in the morning, gentle stretching exercises after lunch, or a dance session to their favorite music can all make a difference. As their strength and endurance improve, gradually increase the duration and intensity of the activities.

Consider incorporating social elements into exercise routines. Joining a walking group, attending a senior fitness class, or simply taking a stroll with a friend or family member can enhance motivation and provide social interaction, which is also crucial for brain health.

It's crucial to adapt exercise routines to your loved one's abilities and preferences. If they have mobility limitations, consider chair exercises or water aerobics. If they enjoy music, incorporate dancing or rhythmic movements. If they prefer outdoor activities, take them for nature walks or gardening. The key is to make exercise enjoyable and accessible so they're more likely to stick with it.

Be mindful of safety considerations. Ensure that your loved one wears comfortable clothing and supportive shoes. Choose activities that are appropriate for their physical condition and avoid any exercises that put them at risk of falls or injuries. If necessary, provide assistance or supervision during exercise sessions.

Remember, consistency is key. Aim for at least 30 minutes of moderate-intensity exercise most days of the week. However, even small amounts of physical activity can make a difference. Encourage your loved one to move throughout the day, even if it's just standing up and stretching or walking around the house.

Physical exercise is not just a prescription for physical health; it's a powerful tool for nurturing the mind and spirit. By incorporating regular activity into your loved one's routine, you can help them maintain cognitive function, improve mood, and enhance their overall quality of life. It's a gift of love, a way to celebrate their strength and resilience, and a testament to the enduring power of the human spirit.

MENTAL WELLNESS AND COGNITIVE EXERCISES FOR DEMENTIA: NURTURING THE MIND

In dementia care, tending to mental wellness and cognitive stimulation is as vital as physical health. It's about nurturing the mind, fostering engagement, and preserving the spark of intellectual curiosity that resides within your loved one. While dementia may gradually dim the light of memory and cognition, it doesn't extinguish the flame entirely. With the right approach, we can stoke that flame, creating moments of connection, joy, and intellectual stimulation that enrich the lives of those with dementia.

Mental wellness encompasses many factors, including emotional well-being, social interaction, and cognitive engagement. For individuals with dementia, maintaining mental health is crucial for managing symptoms, enhancing quality of life, and fostering a sense of purpose and belonging.

Cognitive exercises are one of the most effective ways to promote mental wellness. These activities are designed to challenge the brain, stimulate cognitive functions, and slow the progression of cognitive decline. Think of them as mental workouts, strengthening the neural pathways and fostering new connections.

Various cognitive exercises can be incorporated into your loved one's daily routine. Puzzles, word games, trivia, and memory exercises can all provide mental stimulation and challenge. Choose activities that are appropriate for their cognitive abilities and interests, and be patient if they struggle or become frustrated. The goal is to create an enjoyable and engaging experience, not to test or evaluate their performance.

Reading aloud or silently can also be a wonderful way to stimulate the mind and evoke memories. Choose books or magazines that align with your loved one's interests and be prepared to offer assistance or read aloud if needed. Discussing the content can further enhance cognitive engagement and foster meaningful conversations.

Creative activities like painting, drawing, or writing can also provide mental stimulation and a sense of accomplishment. These activities tap into different parts of the brain, promoting creativity, self-expression, and a sense of control. Focus on something other than the end product; the process of creating is what matters most. Encourage your loved one to explore different mediums and express themselves freely.

Learning new skills or revisiting old hobbies can also be mentally stimulating. Perhaps your loved one always wanted to learn a new language, play a musical instrument, or take up a craft. Explore these interests together, providing encouragement and support along the way. Learning and mastering new skills can boost confidence, self-esteem, and overall cognitive function.

Social interaction is another vital component of mental wellness. Encourage your loved one to take part in social activities, such as visiting with friends and family, attending community events, or joining a support group. These interactions can provide a sense of belonging, reduce isolation, and foster a sense of purpose. Even simple conversations or shared activities can have a profound impact on emotional well-being. Brodaty and Arasaratnam (2012).

Finally, don't underestimate the power of reminiscence. Talking about past experiences, sharing stories, and looking at old photographs can evoke positive emotions and stimulate memory. These conversations can also provide valuable insights into your loved one's life, values, and dreams. Reminiscing can be a powerful way to connect on a deeper level and create a sense of shared history.

Nurturing mental wellness in dementia care is an ongoing process that requires patience, creativity, and a deep understanding of your loved one's needs and preferences. Incorporating cognitive exercises, creative activities, social interaction, and reminiscence into their daily routine can foster engagement, joy, and purpose. Remember, it's not about reversing the effects of dementia but about creating moments of connection and celebrating the personhood of your loved one, even as the disease progresses.

Remember, the goal is to create a rich and fulfilling life for your loved one, one that honors their past, embraces their present, and fosters a sense of hope and possibility for the future. By nurturing their mental wellness, you're not just managing a disease but celebrating a life.

INTEGRATING TECHNOLOGY: APPS AND DEVICES FOR DEMENTIA CARE

In an era where technology permeates nearly every aspect of our lives, it's no surprise that it's also playing an increasingly vital role in dementia care. Orman and Tierney (2018) point out, technology offers a wealth of opportunities to enhance the lives of people with dementia. From smartphone apps that gently remind us of appointments to wearable devices that track our loved ones' movements and even smart home systems that adapt to their changing needs, technology offers a wealth of tools and resources that can significantly enhance the lives of individuals with dementia and their caregivers. It's about harnessing the power of innovation to create a more supportive, safe, and connected environment, where technology acts as a bridge, not a barrier, to a fulfilling life.

Think of technology as a toolbox filled with gadgets and gizmos specifically designed to address the unique challenges of dementia care. These tools can assist with everything from medication management and communication to safety monitoring and cognitive stimulation. They can provide a sense of security, peace of mind, and even moments of joy and connection, easing the burden on caregivers and empowering individuals with dementia to maintain their independence for as long as possible.

One of the most common and practical uses of technology in dementia care is for medication management. Forgetting to take medications or taking incorrect dosages can have serious health consequences. Medication reminder apps, with their gentle alarms and personalized schedules, can help ensure that medications are taken on time and in the correct amounts, reducing the risk of adverse events and hospitalizations. Smart pill dispensers can go a step further, dispensing medications at pre-programmed times and even sending alerts to caregivers if a dose is missed.

GPS trackers and wearable devices can be invaluable for individuals who are prone to wandering, a common behavior in dementia that can lead to anxiety and safety concerns. These devices, often discreetly embedded in watches or pendants, can provide real-time location tracking, allowing caregivers to quickly locate their loved ones if they wander off. Some devices even have geofencing capabilities, sending alerts if the individual leaves a designated safe zone, providing an added layer of security and peace of mind.

Communication can become increasingly challenging as dementia progresses, but technology offers innovative solutions to bridge the gap. Video calling apps can facilitate face-to-face interactions with loved ones, even when physical distance separates them. Simplified communication devices with large buttons and clear icons can help individuals express their needs and desires, even when verbal communication becomes difficult. These tools can foster a sense of connection, reduce isolation, and provide a much-needed emotional boost for both the individual with dementia and their caregivers.

Smart home systems are transforming how we interact with our living spaces, and they can be particularly beneficial for individuals with dementia. Motion sensors can detect falls or unusual activity, alerting caregivers to potential problems. Smart lighting can adjust automatically based on the time of day or occupancy, reducing confusion and promoting safety. Voice-activated assistants can provide reminders for daily tasks, such as taking medications or turning off appliances, fostering independence and reducing caregiver burden.

Beyond safety and daily living support, technology also offers a wealth of opportunities for cognitive stimulation and brain training. Apps and games designed specifically for individuals with dementia can help them maintain mental function, improve memory, and even learn new skills. From puzzles and word games to virtual reality experiences and interactive music programs, these tools offer a fun and engaging way to challenge the brain and promote mental well-being. They can provide a sense of accomplishment, boost self-esteem, and foster a sense of joy and connection.

While technology holds immense promise in dementia care, it's crucial to approach it with thoughtful consideration. Not every tool will be suitable for every individual, and it's important to choose devices and apps that align with your loved one's specific needs, abilities, and preferences. Some individuals may resist new technology or find it overwhelming, so start with simple, user-friendly options and gradually introduce more complex tools as needed.

It's also essential to ensure that technology is used ethically and respectfully. Privacy concerns, data security, and the potential for overreliance on technology are all important considerations. Always involve your loved one in the decision-making process, respect their autonomy, and prioritize their comfort and well-being.

Remember, technology is just one tool in the dementia care toolbox. It can't replace the human connection, compassion, and personalized care that are essential for individuals with dementia. However, when used thoughtfully and appropriately, technology can enhance safety, promote independence, and improve the quality of life for both individuals with dementia and their caregivers. It's about embracing the possibilities of innovation while always focusing on the human heart at the center of care.

THE THERAPEUTIC POWER OF MUSIC AND ART: UNLOCKING THE HEART AND MIND

In dementia care, where words often falter and memories fade, music and art emerge as powerful allies, capable of unlocking hidden emotions, sparking joy, and fostering a sense of connection. They offer a language that transcends the limitations of cognitive decline, a universal language that speaks to the heart and soul. As caregivers, we can harness the therapeutic power of these creative expressions to create moments of shared beauty, ignite memories, and nurture the spirit of our loved ones.

Music, with its rhythm, melody, and emotional resonance, has a profound impact on the human brain. It can evoke memories, trigger emotions, and even stimulate movement and coordination. For individuals with dementia, music can be a lifeline, transporting them back to cherished moments from their past, stirring feelings of joy, nostalgia, and even a sense of self.

Consider creating personalized playlists filled with your loved one's favorite songs from their youth or special occasions. Sing along together, tap your feet to the beat, or sit and listen to the music that once filled their lives with meaning. You might be surprised by the memories that surface, the stories that unfold, and the emotions that come to life.

Music therapy, led by trained professionals, can be particularly beneficial for individuals with dementia. These sessions often involve singing, playing instruments, listening to music, and even movement or dance. Music therapy can improve mood, reduce agitation, and enhance communication and social interaction. It can also provide a sense of accomplishment and self-expression, fostering a sense of purpose and well-being.

Art, in its various forms, can also be a powerful tool for engagement and self-expression. Encourage your loved one to paint, draw, sculpt, or engage in other forms of artistic creation. Creating can be therapeutic, allowing for self-expression, emotional release, and a sense of control. Focus on something other than the end product; the process of creating is what matters most.

Art therapy, facilitated by a trained therapist, can provide a safe and supportive space for individuals with dementia to explore their creativity and express their emotions. Through various art mediums, they can tap into their inner world, communicate their feelings, and connect with others on a deeper level. Art therapy can also improve cognitive function, reduce anxiety, and enhance self-esteem.

The benefits of music and art extend beyond emotional well-being. Studies have shown that these creative expressions can also positively affect cognitive function. Music can stimulate memory recall, improve attention, and even enhance language skills. Art can promote problem-solving, creativity, and fine motor skills. These activities can help individuals with dementia maintain their cognitive abilities for as long as possible and experience a sense of accomplishment and purpose. This is confirmed in research by Särkämö et al. (2008).

As a caregiver, incorporating music and art into your loved one's daily routine can be a source of joy and connection. Sing their favorite songs together, dance in the living room, or create a collaborative art project. Visit museums, attend concerts, listen to music, or admire artwork together. These shared experiences can foster a sense of intimacy, create lasting memories, and remind you both of the beauty and resilience of the human spirit.

Remember, music and art are not just hobbies or pastimes but powerful tools for healing, connection, and self-expression. By embracing these creative outlets, you can nurture your loved one's heart and mind, providing them with moments of joy, peace, and a sense of belonging. Even as dementia challenges their cognitive abilities, music and art can tap into the depths of their soul, reminding them of the beauty and wonder that still exists in the world.

THE HEALING POWER OF NATURE: OUTDOOR ACTIVITIES AND DEMENTIA

In the journey of dementia care, nature emerges as a gentle yet potent source of healing, offering solace, stimulation, and a strong sense of connection to the world. Stepping outside, breathing in the fresh air, and feeling the sun's warmth can awaken the senses, stir memories, and ignite a spark of joy within your loved one. It's about embracing the restorative power of the natural world, recognizing its ability to soothe the mind, uplift the spirit, and foster a sense of well-being even amidst the challenges of cognitive decline.

Imagine strolling through a park, hand-in-hand with your loved one, surrounded by the vibrant colors of blooming flowers and the gentle rustling of leaves. The sun's rays filter through the canopy, casting a dappled light on the path ahead. Birds sing their cheerful melodies, and a gentle breeze carries the scent of freshly cut grass. In this moment, worries fade, and a sense of peace settles over you both.

For individuals with dementia, spending time in nature can be a transformative experience. The natural world's sights, sounds, and smells can evoke memories, stimulate the senses, and promote a sense of calm and well-being. Studies have shown that exposure to nature can reduce agitation, improve mood, and enhance cognitive function in individuals with dementia. It can also promote physical activity, improve sleep quality, and boost overall health. It's like opening a window to a world of sensory experiences that can awaken dormant memories and emotions, fostering a sense of connection to the world and to oneself.

The beauty of nature is its accessibility and versatility. Whether it's a leisurely walk in the park, a picnic in the backyard, or simply sitting on a porch swing and listening to the birds sing, there are countless ways to incorporate outdoor activities into your loved one's routine.

Gardening can be a particularly rewarding activity for individuals with dementia. Planting seeds, nurturing plants, and witnessing the fruits of their labor can provide a sense of purpose and accomplishment. Gardening also offers sensory stimulation through the textures of soil and plants, the vibrant colors of flowers, and the fragrant scents of herbs and blossoms. It's a gentle form of exercise that promotes physical activity and can even improve balance and coordination. Digging in the dirt, tending to plants, and watching them grow can bring a sense of satisfaction and connection to the natural world.

Walking is another excellent way to enjoy the outdoors and reap the benefits of nature. Choose a safe and familiar route and adjust the pace and distance to your loved one's abilities. Walking can improve cardiovascular health, strengthen muscles, and enhance mood. It can also provide an opportunity for conversation, reminiscing, and shared experiences. The rhythmic movement of walking can be soothing, and the changing scenery can provide visual stimulation and a sense of adventure.

If your loved one enjoys animals, consider visiting a petting zoo or spending time with a therapy animal. Interacting with animals can be incredibly soothing and therapeutic, reducing anxiety, lowering blood pressure, and promoting a sense of calm. An animal's unconditional love and companionship can also foster a sense of connection and belonging. The soft fur, the gentle nuzzles, the wagging tail - these simple interactions can bring a smile to their face and warmth to their heart.

For those with limited mobility, simply sitting outdoors and enjoying the sights and sounds of nature can be beneficial. Set up a comfortable chair in a shaded area, listen to the wind rustling through the trees, and watch the birds flitting about. The simple act of being present in nature can be incredibly grounding and restorative. The warmth of the sun, the gentle breeze, and the sounds of nature can create a sense of peace and tranquility, offering a respite from the confines of indoor living.

As you plan outdoor activities, be mindful of safety considerations. Ensure that your loved one wears appropriate clothing and footwear, applies sunscreen, and stays hydrated. Choose activities suitable for their physical abilities and avoid strenuous or risky endeavors. If necessary, provide assistance or supervision to ensure their safety and well-being. Remember, the goal is to create enjoyable and meaningful experiences that connect your loved one with the natural world. Be flexible, adaptable, and responsive to their needs and preferences. Celebrate the moments of joy, laughter, and connection that emerge amidst the challenges of dementia.

By embracing the healing power of nature, you can nurture your loved one's spirit, stimulate their senses, and create a sense of peace and well-being. It's a testament to the enduring beauty of the world around us and the resilience of the human spirit, even in the face of adversity.

"A good laugh and a long sleep are the two best cures for anything." — *Irish Proverb*

5

LEGAL, FINANCIAL, AND FUTURE CARE PLANNING

In the realm of dementia care, where the unpredictable currents of cognitive decline can swiftly alter the course of one's life, the concept of Power of Attorney emerges as a tool of preparedness and protection. It's a legal document that empowers you, as a trusted caregiver, to make crucial decisions on behalf of your loved one when they can no longer do so themselves. Think of it as a safety net, ensuring that their wishes are respected, their finances are managed responsibly, and their well-being is safeguarded, even as the fog of dementia thickens. (Alzheimer's Association. (2023). Legal documents. Retrieve from https://www.alz.org/help-support/caregiving/financial-legal-planning/legal-documents).

At its core, the Power of Attorney is a legal document that grants authority to another person, known as the agent or attorney-in-fact, to act on behalf of the principal, the individual granting the power. This authority can encompass a wide range of decisions, including financial matters, healthcare choices, and even legal affairs. It's a profound act of trust, entrusting someone you deeply care about with the responsibility of making decisions that will shape your loved one's future.

There are two primary types of Power of Attorney relevant to dementia care:

1. <u>Durable Power of Attorney for Healthcare</u>: This type of Power of Attorney specifically addresses healthcare decisions, allowing the agent to make choices about medical treatment, hospitalization, and end-of-life care when the principal is no longer capable of doing so. It ensures that your loved one's wishes regarding their healthcare are honored, even if they are unable to communicate them directly.

2. <u>Durable Power of Attorney for Finances</u>: This type of Power of Attorney focuses on financial matters, granting the agent the authority to manage bank accounts, pay bills, file taxes, and make other financial decisions on behalf of the principal. It provides a safeguard against asset exploitation and ensures that your loved one's financial affairs are handled responsibly and in their best interests.

Establishing Power of Attorney is a proactive step that can bring peace of mind and prevent potential complications down the road. It's best to initiate this process early in the dementia journey while your loved one still has the cognitive capacity to understand and make informed decisions. Delaying this important step can lead to legal hurdles, family disputes, and unnecessary stress during an already challenging time.

When establishing Power of Attorney, it's crucial to choose an agent who is trustworthy, responsible, and capable of handling the responsibilities involved. This person should be someone who understands your loved one's values, wishes, and preferences and who will always act in their best interests. It's also important to communicate openly with your chosen agent, ensuring they understand the scope of their authority and your expectations.

Establishing Power of Attorney typically involves consulting an attorney to draft the legal documents. The attorney will explain the different types of Power of Attorney, their limitations, and the specific requirements for your state or jurisdiction. They can also help you tailor the documents to your loved one's needs and circumstances.

Once the documents are prepared, your loved one will need to sign them in the presence of witnesses and a notary public. It's essential to ensure they fully understand the implications of granting Power of Attorney and do so voluntarily.

Remember, Power of Attorney is not a one-size-fits-all solution. It's a legal tool that should be customized to your loved one's needs and circumstances. By understanding the different types of Power of Attorney, choosing the right agent, and establishing these documents early on, you can safeguard your loved one's future and ensure their wishes are respected, even as dementia progresses. It's a proactive step that can bring peace of mind and empower you to navigate the complexities of dementia care with confidence and compassion.

LEGAL DOCUMENTS EVERY CAREGIVER SHOULD KNOW ABOUT

When dementia enters your loved one's life, it also enters the realm of legal and financial matters. It's crucial to be prepared with the necessary legal documents to ensure your loved one's wishes are respected, their assets are protected, and their care is managed effectively. Navigating this paper trail might seem daunting, but understanding these key documents can provide peace of mind and prevent potential complications down the road.

Beyond the Power of Attorney documents discussed in the previous subchapter, several other legal documents are essential for caregivers to be aware of:

- <u>Advance Directive for Healthcare</u>: Also known as a living will, this document outlines your loved one's wishes regarding medical treatment in situations where they can no longer communicate their preferences. It can include instructions about life-sustaining treatments, pain management, and organ donation. Having an advance directive in place ensures that your loved one's values and beliefs are respected, even if they are unable to express them directly.
- <u>Do Not Resuscitate (DNR) Order</u>: This medical order instructs healthcare providers not to perform cardiopulmonary resuscitation (CPR) if your loved one's heart stops or they stop breathing. It's a personal decision that should be made in consultation with your loved one, their doctor, and family members.
- <u>Physician Orders for Life-Sustaining Treatment</u> (<u>POLST</u>): This medical order complements an advance directive by providing specific instructions for current medical treatments. It's a portable document that travels with your loved one and guides healthcare professionals in various settings, such as hospitals, nursing homes, and even at home.
- <u>Will</u>: A will is a legal document outlining how your loved one's assets will be distributed after death. It's essential to have an updated will in place to ensure that their wishes are carried out and to avoid potential disputes among family members.

- <u>Trust</u>: A trust is a legal arrangement where a trustee holds and manages assets for the benefit of another person, known as the beneficiary. Trusts can be used for various purposes, such as protecting assets from creditors, minimizing estate taxes, or providing for a loved one with special needs.
- <u>HIPAA Authorization Form</u>: The Health Insurance Portability and Accountability Act (HIPAA) protects the privacy of medical information. A HIPAA authorization form allows you to access your loved one's medical records and communicate with their healthcare providers on their behalf.

Having these legal documents in place can simplify the complexities of dementia care and ensure that your loved one's wishes are respected at every stage of the journey. It's essential to review these documents regularly, update them as needed, and keep copies in a safe and accessible location. Consider sharing copies with trusted family members or healthcare providers so they are aware of your loved one's wishes.

Navigating the legal and financial aspects of dementia care can be overwhelming, but it's crucial to providing compassionate and responsible care. Don't hesitate to seek guidance from an elder law attorney or financial advisor specializing in dementia care. They can help you understand the legal landscape, create the necessary documents, and ensure that your loved one's interests are protected.

Remember, these legal documents are not just about paperwork; they are about empowering your loved one and ensuring their voice is heard, even when they can no longer speak for themselves. By taking proactive steps to prepare these documents, you can navigate the challenges of dementia care with confidence, knowing that you're honoring your loved one's wishes and safeguarding their future.

NAVIGATING FINANCIAL PLANNING AND ASSISTANCE FOR DEMENTIA CARE

Dementia, with its relentless progression and often unpredictable course, can place a significant financial burden on individuals and their families. The cost of medications, therapies, home care services, and potentially long-term care facilities can quickly add up, creating a sense of anxiety and uncertainty about the future. However, with careful planning and a proactive approach, you must try to navigate the financial complexities of dementia care and ensure that your loved one's needs are met while also protecting your own financial well-being. (National Institute on Aging. (2023). Managing Money Problems for People With Dementia. Retrieve from https://www. nia.nih.gov/health/legal-and-financial-planning/managing-money-problems-people-dementia).

The first step in financial planning is to assess your loved one's current situation. Gather information about their income sources, assets, debts, and insurance coverage. This will provide a clear picture of their financial resources and help you identify any potential gaps or challenges.

Next, create a budget for current and future care expenses. This includes costs for medications, therapies, home care services, medical equipment, transportation, and potential long-term care. Be realistic about the likely costs and factors in inflation and the possibility of increased care needs as dementia progresses.

Explore available financial assistance programs. Many government programs, non-profit organizations, and private foundations offer financial assistance for dementia care. These programs may cover the cost of medications, home care services, respite care, and even long-term care facilities. Research these programs thoroughly and determine if your loved one qualifies for benefits.

Consider long-term care insurance. This type of insurance can help cover the cost of long-term care services, such as assisted living or nursing home care. While it can be expensive, it can also provide significant financial protection and peace of mind. If your loved one already has long-term care insurance, review the policy carefully to understand the coverage and benefits.

Consult with a financial advisor who specializes in elder care. They can help you develop a comprehensive financial plan that addresses your loved one's current and future needs. They can also provide guidance on tax implications, estate planning, and investment strategies.

Be mindful of potential scams and financial exploitation. Unfortunately, individuals with dementia are particularly vulnerable to fraud and exploitation. Be cautious about unsolicited offers, high-pressure sales tactics, and personal or financial information requests. If you suspect any fraudulent activity, report it to the authorities immediately.

Encourage your loved one to participate in financial decision-making as long as they are able. This can help them maintain a sense of control and autonomy and facilitate open communication and trust within the family.

As dementia progresses, you may need to assume more responsibility for managing your loved one's finances. Use Power of Attorney for Finances wisely and responsibly, always acting in your loved one's best interests. Keep meticulous records of all financial transactions and consult a financial advisor or attorney with any questions or concerns.

Remember, financial planning for dementia care is not just about numbers; it's about ensuring that your loved one's needs are met and their dignity is preserved. By taking a proactive approach, exploring available resources, and seeking professional guidance, you can create a secure financial foundation that will support your loved one throughout their journey. It's about creating peace of mind, knowing that their economic well-being is protected and that they can access the care they need, regardless of the challenges that lie ahead.

TRANSITIONING TO ASSISTED LIVING OR MEMORY CARE: MAKING THE DECISION

The decision to transition your loved one from their familiar home to an assisted living or memory care facility is often one of the most challenging and emotionally charged choices a caregiver faces. It's a crossroads where love, practicality, and a deep sense of responsibility converge, leaving you grappling with questions of safety, independence, and quality of life. It's a decision that requires careful consideration, open communication, and a willingness to prioritize your loved one's well-being above all else.

For many caregivers, the idea of moving their loved one out of their home can be a source of guilt, sadness, and a sense of loss. It can feel like a betrayal of trust, giving up control, or even an admission of defeat. These emotions are valid and understandable. After all, home is often a sanctuary, a place filled with memories, comfort, and a sense of belonging. The prospect of uprooting your loved one from this familiar environment can be heart-wrenching.

However, it's important to remember that the primary goal is to ensure your loved one's safety, well-being, and quality of life. As dementia progresses, the challenges of caregiving can become overwhelming, even for the most dedicated and loving families. Your loved one may require 24-hour supervision, specialized care, or assistance with activities of daily living that you are no longer able to provide at home. In these situations, transitioning to an assisted living or memory care facility can be the most compassionate and responsible choice.

Assisted living facilities offer a supportive environment where individuals with mild to moderate dementia can maintain their independence while receiving assistance with daily tasks, such as medication management, meals, and personal care. These facilities often provide social activities, transportation, and other amenities that can enhance quality of life and reduce isolation.

Memory care facilities, on the other hand, are specifically designed for individuals with more advanced dementia. They offer a secure and structured environment with specialized staff trained in dementia care. These facilities often have enhanced safety features, such as secure entrances and exits, and provide a range of activities and therapies tailored to the needs of individuals with memory impairment.

Making the decision to transition your loved one to an assisted living or memory care facility takes work. It's a complex process that involves balancing various factors, including your loved one's needs, your own capabilities as a caregiver, financial considerations, and the availability of suitable facilities in your area. It's essential to gather information, visit different facilities, and talk to staff members and other residents to understand the environment and the level of care provided.

It's also crucial to involve your loved one in the decision-making process as much as possible. Explain the reasons for considering a move, address their concerns, and reassure them that you will continue to be involved in their care. While they may initially resist the idea, involving them in the process can help ease the transition and promote a sense of autonomy.

Once the decision is made, approach the move with sensitivity and compassion. Pack familiar belongings, decorate their new space with personal items, and maintain a consistent routine as much as possible. Visit frequently, participate in activities, and continue to express your love and support.

Remember, transitioning to an assisted living or memory care facility is not a sign of failure or abandonment. It's a courageous and loving decision that prioritizes your loved one's well-being and ensures they receive the specialized care they need. It's about creating a safe and supportive environment where they can continue to live a meaningful life, surrounded by compassionate caregivers and engaging activities.

END-OF-LIFE CARE: CONVERSATIONS AND PLANNING

Dementia, like any terminal illness, inevitably leads to the final chapter of life. While it can be difficult to contemplate this reality, having open and honest conversations about end-of-life care is crucial for ensuring your loved one's wishes are respected and that their final days are filled with comfort, dignity, and peace. It's a time for reflection, expressing love and gratitude, and making decisions that honor their values and beliefs.

Initiating these conversations may seem daunting, but it's important to remember that they are an act of love and respect. By discussing end-of-life care preferences early on, while your loved one still has the cognitive capacity to participate, you can alleviate anxiety, prevent misunderstandings, and ensure their voice is heard. These conversations are not about dwelling on death but about celebrating life and ensuring that its final chapter is as meaningful and fulfilling as possible.

Start by creating a safe and comfortable space for these conversations. Choose a time when your loved one is relaxed and receptive and approach the topic with sensitivity and compassion. Be prepared to listen actively, validate their feelings, and address any concerns they may have.

Some key topics to discuss include:

- Advance directives: These legal documents outline your loved one's wishes regarding medical treatment in situations where they are no longer able to communicate their preferences. Discuss their preferences for life-sustaining treatments, pain management, and organ donation.
- Palliative care: This specialized medical care focuses on relieving the symptoms and stress of a severe illness like dementia. Discuss the benefits of palliative care, which can enhance comfort, improve quality of life, and provide emotional and spiritual support for both the individual and their family.
- Hospice care: This type of care is provided in the final stages of life, focusing on comfort and quality of life rather than curative treatments. Discuss the philosophy of hospice care, its benefits, and how it can support your loved one and your family during this difficult time.
- Funeral and burial arrangements: While this may be a sensitive topic, discussing your loved one's preferences for their funeral or memorial service can provide peace of mind and ensure their final wishes are honored.

As you navigate these conversations, remember that feeling a range of emotions is okay. You might experience sadness, fear, or even guilt. It's important to acknowledge these feelings and seek support from family, friends, or a therapist if needed. Remember, you're not alone in this journey.

It's also important to be flexible and adaptable. Your loved one's wishes may change over time, and revisiting these conversations as needed is okay. The goal is to ensure their preferences are respected and their final days are filled with love, comfort, and dignity.

End-of-life planning is not just about making decisions; it's also about creating opportunities for closure, forgiveness, and expressions of love. Spend time reminiscing, sharing stories, and expressing gratitude for your time together. These moments of connection can be incredibly healing and provide a sense of peace as you navigate the final chapter of your loved one's life.

Remember, end-of-life care is not about giving up; it's about embracing the natural cycle of life and ensuring that your loved one's final days are filled with love, comfort, and dignity. By having open and honest conversations, planning ahead, and seeking support, you can create a peaceful and meaningful ending to their journey. It's a testament to the enduring power of love, the beauty of shared memories, and the grace that can be found even in the face of loss.

PRESERVING DIGNITY IN LATE-STAGE DEMENTIA CARE

As dementia progresses into its later stages, the challenges of caregiving intensify, and the focus shifts from managing symptoms to providing comfort, dignity, and unwavering love. It's a time of extreme vulnerability, where your loved one may be unable to communicate their needs, recognize familiar faces, or even perform basic tasks. In these moments, preserving their dignity becomes paramount, a testament to the enduring value of their life and the depth of your compassion.

Preserving dignity in late-stage dementia care is not just about meeting physical needs; it's about honoring the personhood of your loved one, recognizing their inherent worth, and treating them with respect and tenderness. It's about creating an environment where they feel safe, secure, and loved, even as the world around them fades.

One of the most important aspects of preserving dignity is maintaining a sense of control and autonomy. Even in the later stages of dementia, individuals can still express preferences and make choices, however limited they may be. Offer choices whenever possible, whether about what to wear, what to eat, or what activities to engage in. Respect their decisions, even if they seem illogical or unconventional. This simple act of allowing them to make choices can foster a sense of empowerment and self-worth.

Communication, even in its most basic forms, remains crucial. While verbal communication may become increasingly difficult, non-verbal cues, such as facial expressions, gestures, and touch, can still convey love, comfort, and understanding. Speak calmly and gently, use simple words and phrases, and maintain eye contact. Even if your loved one doesn't respond verbally, they can still sense your presence and affection.

Personal care routines, such as bathing, dressing, and grooming, require special attention in late-stage dementia. Approach these tasks with the utmost respect and sensitivity, ensuring privacy and minimizing discomfort or embarrassment. Use gentle touch, warm water, and familiar scents to create a soothing and comforting experience. Allow your loved one to participate as much as possible, even if it's just choosing their outfit or brushing their own hair. These small acts of independence can foster a sense of dignity and self-esteem.

Creating a comfortable and familiar environment is also crucial. Surround your loved one with familiar objects, photographs, and mementos that evoke positive memories and emotions. Play their favorite music, read aloud from familiar books, or engage in simple activities they once enjoyed. These familiar sights, sounds, and experiences can provide a sense of comfort and security, even as their cognitive abilities decline.

As dementia progresses, it's important to be mindful of your loved one's physical comfort. Ensure that they are well-nourished, hydrated, and free from pain or discomfort. Please pay attention to their positioning and ensure they are comfortable in bed or in their chair. Regularly check for skin breakdown or other signs of discomfort and address any issues promptly.

End-of-life care is a sensitive and emotional topic, but it's an important part of preserving dignity in late-stage dementia. Discuss your loved one's wishes regarding medical interventions, pain management, and spiritual or religious practices. Ensure that their advance directives are in place and that their healthcare team is aware of their preferences.

Remember, preserving dignity is not just about physical care; it's about honoring the personhood of your loved one and recognizing their inherent value. It's about creating an environment where they feel safe, loved, and respected, even as the challenges of dementia intensify. By approaching caregiving with compassion, empathy, and a focus on maintaining autonomy and connection, you can create a meaningful and fulfilling experience for your loved one, even in the twilight of their life.

"It is not the load that breaks you down. It's the way you carry it." — Lena Horne, singer

6

SELF-CARE AND COPING STRATEGIES FOR CAREGIVERS

In the demanding and emotionally charged world of dementia caregiving, it's all too easy to lose sight of your own needs amidst the constant demands of caring for a loved one. The physical, emotional, and mental toll can be immense, leaving you feeling drained, depleted, and overwhelmed. Sorensen et al. (2006) describe this phenomenon as a state of physical, emotional, and mental exhaustion that can affect caregivers, particularly those caring for loved ones with dementia. Caregiver burnout is a very real and serious condition, and it's essential to recognize its signs and take proactive steps to prevent it. Just as a candle needs a steady flame to continue shining, caregivers need to prioritize their health and happiness to provide sustainable and compassionate care.

Caregiver burnout is a natural consequence of the immense challenges and responsibilities that come with caring for someone with dementia. The constant demands of providing physical care, managing behavioral changes, and navigating the emotional rollercoaster of the disease can take a toll on even the most resilient individuals. Day in and day out, you may find yourself juggling medication schedules, assisting with personal care, dealing with unpredictable behaviors, and grappling with the emotional weight of witnessing your loved one's decline. It's a relentless cycle that can leave you feeling physically and emotionally exhausted.

Recognizing the signs of burnout is the first step toward prevention and recovery. These signs can manifest in various ways, both physically and emotionally. You might experience chronic fatigue, find it difficult to get out of bed in the morning, or be constantly tired throughout the day. Sleep disturbances, such as insomnia or restless sleep, can further exacerbate fatigue and leave you feeling unrested. Changes in appetite, whether eating too much or too little, can also be a sign of burnout.

Physical symptoms may also include frequent headaches, muscle tension, or a weakened immune system, making you more susceptible to illness. Emotionally, you might feel over-whelmed, irritable, anxious, or depressed. You might find your-self withdrawing from social activities, neglecting your own needs, or feeling resentful towards your loved one or your care-giving role. These emotional changes can impact your relation-ships, work, and overall sense of self.

If you recognize any of these signs in yourself, it's vital to take action. Ignoring burnout can lead to serious health conse-quences, both physical and mental. It can also compromise your ability to provide effective and compassionate care for your loved one. When you're running on empty, offering the patience, understanding, and support your loved one needs isn't easy.

Preventing caregiver burnout requires a proactive and holistic approach. It's about recognizing your limitations, setting boundaries, and prioritizing self-care. Just as you wouldn't neglect to refuel your car or recharge your phone, you shouldn't neglect to recharge yourself. Here are some strategies that can help:

- Ask for help: Be bold and reach out to family, friends, or community resources for support. Delegate tasks, share responsibilities, and allow others to help you. Remember, you don't have to do it all alone. It takes a village to care for someone with dementia, and some people are willing and able to help.
- Set realistic expectations: Caregiving is a marathon, not a sprint. Don't expect yourself to be perfect or handle everything alone. Set realistic goals, prioritize tasks, and learn to say no when necessary. It's okay to acknowledge your limitations and ask for help when needed.
- Take breaks: Schedule regular breaks throughout the day, even if it's just for a few minutes. Step outside for fresh air, listen to music, or engage in a relaxing activity. These brief respites can help you recharge and return to your caregiving duties with renewed energy.
- Connect with other caregivers: Join a support group or online forum where you can share your experiences, receive validation, and learn from others who are navigating a similar journey. Knowing that you're not alone can be incredibly empowering and comforting. Sharing your struggles and triumphs with others can provide a sense of community and understanding.
- Prioritize your own health: Make time for regular exercise, eat a healthy diet, and get enough sleep. Taking care of your physical health will enhance your resilience and ability to cope with stress. Remember, you can't care for others if you're not caring for yourself.
- Seek professional help: If you're struggling with anxiety, depression, or other mental health challenges, don't

hesitate to seek professional help. A therapist or counselor can provide support, guidance, and coping strategies. Talking to a professional can help you process your emotions, develop healthy coping mechanisms, and navigate the challenges of caregiving.

By recognizing the signs of caregiver burnout, setting boundaries, and prioritizing self-care, you can prevent its effects and continue to provide compassionate and effective care for your loved one. You are not alone in this journey; resources and support are available to help you navigate the challenges and find moments of joy and connection along the way.

EFFECTIVE STRESS MANAGEMENT TECHNIQUES FOR CAREGIVERS

Caregiving for a loved one with dementia can be a relentless whirlwind of emotions, responsibilities, and challenges. It's a role that demands your time, energy, and compassion, often leaving you feeling stressed, overwhelmed, and emotionally drained. The constant worry, the unpredictable behaviors, the physical demands of caregiving—it can all take a toll on your mental and physical health. But amidst the chaos, there is an oasis of calm, moments of respite where you can recharge, reconnect with yourself, and find the strength to continue this journey. Stress management isn't a luxury; it's a necessity for caregivers.

Stress is a natural response to challenging situations, and caregiving for someone with dementia is undoubtedly one of the most demanding roles you can undertake. However, chronic stress can have detrimental effects on your health, weakening your immune system, increasing your risk of heart disease, and contributing to anxiety and depression. It can also impair your ability to provide adequate care, leading to frustration, impatience, and even resentment.

Recognizing the signs of stress is crucial. These signs can manifest in various ways, both physical and emotional. You might experience muscle tension, headaches, digestive problems, or changes in sleep patterns. Emotionally, you might feel overwhelmed, irritable, anxious, or withdrawn. You might need help concentrating, making decisions, or enjoying activities you once loved.

Once you recognize the signs of stress, taking proactive steps to manage it is essential. There are a variety of effective stress management techniques that can help you find calm in the chaos, restore balance to your life, and nurture your own well-being.

Mindfulness and meditation exercises can be potent tools for stress reduction. Taking a few minutes each day to focus on your breath, observe your thoughts and feelings without judgment, and cultivate a sense of inner peace can profoundly impact your overall well-being. Mindfulness can help you stay grounded in the present moment, reducing anxiety and promoting a sense of calm even during challenging situations.

Exercise is another excellent way to manage stress and boost your mood. Physical activity releases endorphins, natural mood boosters that can help combat feelings of anxiety and depression. It also promotes relaxation, improves sleep quality, and enhances overall physical health. Find activities you enjoy, whether it's walking, swimming, yoga, or dancing, and incorporate them into your routine.

Connecting with others is essential for stress management. Talk to friends, family members, or other caregivers about your experiences and feelings. Sharing your burdens can lighten the load and provide a sense of validation and support. Consider joining a support group or online forum where you can connect with others who understand the unique challenges of dementia caregiving.

Creative outlets, such as writing, painting, or playing music, can also be therapeutic. Expressing your emotions through creative expression can help you process your feelings, reduce stress, and find moments of joy and inspiration. It's a way to connect with your inner self and tap into your creative spirit, even during challenging circumstances.

Finally, take into account the power of laughter. Humor can be a powerful antidote to stress, providing a much-needed release and perspective. Watch a funny movie, share jokes with friends, or find the humor in everyday situations. Laughter can lighten your mood, reduce tension, and remind you of the joy and beauty in the world.

Remember, stress management is not a one-size-fits-all approach. Experiment with different techniques and find what works best for you. Be patient with yourself, and don't be afraid to ask for help when you need it. By prioritizing your own well-being, you'll be better equipped to navigate the challenges of caregiving and provide the compassionate support your loved one deserves.

BUILDING RESILIENCE IN CAREGIVERS: STRATEGIES FOR EMOTIONAL STRENGTH

In the face of the relentless challenges of dementia caregiving, resilience becomes a precious guard, shielding the heart and mind from the inevitable storms that arise along the way. It's the ability to bend without breaking, adapt to the disease's ever-changing landscape, and emerge from the depths of despair with renewed strength and determination. Building resilience is not about denying the difficulties or pretending everything is fine; it's about cultivating a deep source of inner strength, a reservoir of hope and optimism that sustains you through the darkest times.

Resilience is not an innate trait; it's a skill that can be nurtured and developed over time. It's about cultivating a mindset that embraces challenges as opportunities for growth, recognizing your own strengths and limitations, and finding meaning and purpose amid adversity. It's about learning to navigate the emotional rollercoaster of caregiving, to find moments of peace and joy even in the face of loss, and to emerge from the experience with a deeper sense of compassion and understanding.

One of the key pillars of resilience is self-awareness. Take the time to reflect on your own emotions, thoughts, and behaviors. Recognize your triggers, your coping mechanisms, and your limits. By understanding yourself better, you can identify areas where you need to build resilience and develop strategies to manage stress and maintain your emotional well-being.

Another crucial aspect of resilience is cultivating a positive mindset. This doesn't mean ignoring the challenges or pretending that everything is perfect. It's about choosing to focus on the positive aspects of your life, celebrating small victories, and finding gratitude amid adversity. Practice positive self-talk, challenge negative thoughts, and surround yourself with supportive people who uplift and encourage you.

Building strong connections with others is also essential for resilience. Reach out to family, friends, and other caregivers for support. Please share your experiences, express your feelings, and ask for help when you need it. Joining a support group or online community can provide a safe space to connect with others who understand the unique challenges of dementia caregiving. These connections can offer a lifeline, providing emotional support, practical advice, and a sense of belonging.

Self-care is not a luxury; it's a necessity for caregivers. Make time for activities like reading, listening to music, spending time in nature, or pursuing a hobby. Prioritize your physical health by eating nutritious meals, exercising regularly, and getting enough sleep. These self-care practices can help you recharge, reduce stress, and maintain your emotional and physical well-being.

Finally, remember that seeking professional help shows you are strong, not weak. If you're struggling with anxiety, depression, or other mental health challenges, don't hesitate to reach out to a therapist or counselor. They can provide support, guidance, and coping strategies to help you navigate the emotional complexities of caregiving.

Building resilience is an ongoing process, and it requires dedication and commitment. But the rewards are immeasurable. By cultivating emotional strength, you can navigate the challenges of dementia caregiving with grace and resilience. You can find moments of joy and connection amidst the difficulties and emerge from the experience with a deeper sense of compassion, gratitude, and love. Remember, you are not alone in this journey. By nurturing your own well-being, you are also nurturing the well-being of your loved one, creating a legacy of love and resilience that will endure long after the final chapter of their life.

THE IMPORTANCE OF BUILDING A CAREGIVER SUPPORT NETWORK: STRENGTH IN SHARED EXPERIENCES

In the demanding and emotionally charged journey of dementia caregiving, it's easy to feel isolated and alone. The weight of responsibility, the constant demands on your time and energy, and the emotional toll of witnessing your loved one's decline can leave you feeling overwhelmed and disconnected from the world. However, building a solid support network can be a lifeline, providing a sense of community, understanding, and shared strength. It's about recognizing that you're not alone in this journey and that others understand your struggles, fears, and triumphs.

A support network can take many forms, from close family and friends to formal support groups and online communities. It's about surrounding yourself with people who care about you, listen without judgment, and offer encouragement and practical assistance. These connections can provide a safe space to express your emotions, share your experiences, and receive the validation and understanding you need to navigate the challenges of caregiving. For support group information, contact <u>Alzheimer's and Dementia Support Groups</u> (alzfdn.org).

Family members can be a crucial source of support. They can offer practical help with tasks like grocery shopping, meal preparation, or transportation. They can also provide emotional support, listen to your concerns, offer words of encouragement, and simply be there to share the burden. Open communication and honest conversations about your needs and expectations can help foster a collaborative and supportive dynamic within the family.

Friends can also play a vital role in your support network. They can offer a listening ear, a shoulder to cry on, or a much-needed break from the demands of caregiving. Feel free to reach out to friends and let them know how they can help. Even simple gestures, like bringing a meal or offering to spend time with your loved one, can make a difference.

Formal support groups, in-person or online, can provide a unique sense of community and understanding. These groups bring together caregivers facing similar challenges, creating a safe space to share experiences, exchange information, and receive emotional support. Hearing the stories of others who have walked a similar path can be incredibly empowering and validating. It reminds you that you're not alone and that there are others who understand the unique complexities of dementia caregiving.

To find support groups in your community, consider contacting local hospitals, senior centers, religious organizations, or the Alzheimer's Association. They often offer a variety of support groups tailored to different needs and stages of the disease. You can also search online for virtual support groups or forums that connect caregivers from all over the world.

Professional support services, such as therapists, counselors, and social workers, can also be crucial to your support network. They can provide individual or family counseling, offer coping strategies for managing stress and anxiety, and help you navigate the emotional complexities of caregiving. Don't hesitate to seek professional help if you're feeling overwhelmed, depressed, or struggling to cope.

Building a support network takes time and effort, but it's an investment that will pay dividends throughout your caregiving journey. Reach out to others, be open about your needs, and don't be afraid to ask for help. Remember, you're not alone in this. By connecting with others, sharing your experiences, and receiving support, you can build resilience, find strength in shared experiences, and navigate the challenges of dementia caregiving with greater ease and grace.

NAVIGATING YOUR EMOTIONAL HEALTH: SEEKING PROFESSIONAL HELP

Caregiving for a loved one with dementia is an act of profound love and devotion, but it can also be an emotional rollercoaster.

As you navigate the complexities of the disease, witnessing the gradual decline of your loved one's cognitive abilities and personality, it's natural to experience a range of emotions, from sadness and grief to frustration and even anger. These emotions are valid and understandable, but if left unaddressed, they can take a toll on your mental health and well-being.

Seeking professional help is a courageous step towards self-care and emotional resilience. It's about recognizing that you're not alone in this journey and that there are trained professionals who can provide support, guidance, and coping strategies to help you navigate the emotional complexities of caregiving. It's about prioritizing your own mental health so you can continue to provide compassionate and effective care for your loved one.

Therapy or counseling can offer a safe and confidential space to explore your feelings, process your grief, and develop healthy coping mechanisms. A therapist can help you understand the normal stages of grief associated with dementia, identify and challenge negative thought patterns, and develop strategies for managing stress and anxiety. They can also provide tools for effective communication, conflict resolution, and self-care.

Support groups, either in-person or online, can also be a valuable resource for emotional support. Connecting with other caregivers who are facing similar challenges can create a sense of community and understanding. Sharing your experiences, listening to others, and receiving validation can be incredibly empowering and comforting. It reminds you that you're not alone in this journey and that others understand what you're going through.

In addition to therapy and support groups, other resources are available to support your emotional health. Mindfulness and meditation sessions can help you cultivate inner peace and resilience. Regular exercise, a healthy diet, and adequate sleep are crucial for maintaining emotional well-being. Remember to appreciate the power of simple self-care practices, such as taking a warm bath, listening to music, or spending time in nature. These small acts of self-kindness can make a big difference in your overall mood and outlook.

If you're experiencing symptoms of depression or anxiety, such as persistent sadness, hopelessness, excessive worry, or panic attacks, it's vital to seek professional help. A mental health professional can assess your symptoms, provide a diagnosis, and recommend appropriate treatment options, which may include therapy, medication, or a combination of both.

Remember, seeking professional help is a sign of self-awareness. It's about recognizing your needs, prioritizing your well-being, and taking proactive steps to manage your emotional health. By addressing your own emotional needs, you'll be better equipped to care for your loved one and to navigate the challenges of dementia with grace and resilience.

Feel free to reach out for help when you need it. There are countless resources available to support you on this journey. Remember, you're not alone. By seeking professional help, connecting with others, and practicing self-care, you can nurture your emotional health, build resilience, and find moments of peace and joy even amid adversity. A wonderful resource is: https://www.nccdp.org/caregiver-stress-syndrome-signs-and-coping-strategies/

BALANCING CAREGIVING WITH WORK AND PERSONAL LIFE: FINDING HARMONY IN THE JUGGLE

Caregiving for a loved one with dementia is a profound act of love, but it's also a demanding responsibility that can strain even the most resilient individuals. Balancing the demands of caregiving with work and personal life responsibilities can feel like an impossible juggling act, leaving you feeling stretched thin, overwhelmed, and constantly on the verge of burnout. But finding harmony in this delicate balance is not only possible but also essential for your own well-being and the sustainability of your caregiving journey.

The first step in achieving this balance is acknowledging the challenges and setting realistic expectations. Caregiving for someone with dementia is not a 9-to-5 job; it's a 24/7 commitment that can disrupt your sleep, your work schedule, and your social life. It's essential to be honest with yourself about the time and energy required and to adjust your expectations accordingly.

If you're employed, talk to your employer about your caregiving responsibilities. Many companies offer flexible work arrangements, such as telecommuting, reduced hours, or compressed workweeks, to help you balance work and caregiving. Explore available leave options, such as the Family and Medical Leave Act (FMLA), which provides eligible employees with up to 12 weeks of unpaid, job-protected leave to care for a family member with a severe health condition.

Delegate tasks and responsibilities whenever possible. Don't try to do it all yourself. Enlist the help of family members, friends, or neighbors. Consider hiring a home health aide or respite care provider to assist with daily tasks and provide you with much-needed breaks. Remember, asking for help is a sign of strength and self-awareness.

Prioritize and simplify your life. Identify the most essential tasks and focus on those. Let go of non-essential activities or commitments that drain your time and energy. Consider using online grocery delivery services, meal preparation services, or other time-saving tools to streamline your daily routine.

Create a schedule that works for you and your loved one. Establish a consistent daily routine incorporating caregiving tasks, work responsibilities, and personal time. Be flexible and adaptable, allowing for unexpected changes or challenges. Remember, it's okay to adjust your schedule as needed to accommodate your loved one's needs and your own well-being.

Make time for self-care. Amidst the demands of caregiving, it's easy to neglect your own needs. But taking care of yourself is not selfish; it's essential for your physical and emotional health. Schedule regular breaks throughout the day, even if it's just for a few minutes. Engage in activities you enjoy, connect with friends and family, and prioritize healthy habits like exercise and sleep.

Set boundaries and communicate them clearly. Establishing boundaries with family members, friends, and even your loved one is important. Let them know your limits and what you're comfortable with. Be bold and say yes to requests or commitments you can't realistically handle. Clear communication can prevent misunderstandings and resentment, fostering a more supportive and collaborative environment.

Remember, finding harmony in the juggle of caregiving, work, and personal life is an ongoing process. It requires constant adjustment, flexibility, and a willingness to prioritize your own well-being. By setting realistic expectations, delegating tasks, simplifying your life, and making time for self-care, you can create a sustainable and fulfilling caregiving experience.

FINDING RESPITE: OPTIONS FOR TAKING NECESSARY BREAKS

In the marathon of dementia caregiving, taking breaks isn't a luxury; it's a necessity. Like a runner needing water stations along the course, caregivers need moments of respite to recharge, refuel, and renew their energy. These breaks, whether brief or extended, can provide a much-needed escape from the demands of caregiving, allowing you to tend to your own physical, emotional, and mental well-being. It's about recognizing that self-care is not selfish; it's essential for sustainable and compassionate care.

Respite care comes in various forms, each offering unique benefits and opportunities for caregivers to step away from their responsibilities, even if just for a short while.

- <u>In-home respite care</u>: This option brings a trained caregiver into your home to provide temporary relief, allowing you to run errands, attend appointments, or relax and recharge. It can be arranged for a few hours, a day, or even overnight, depending on your needs and preferences.
- <u>Adult daycare centers</u>: These centers provide a safe and stimulating environment for individuals with dementia, offering social interaction, activities, and meals. They can be an excellent option for caregivers who need a break during the day or are looking for opportunities for their loved one to socialize and engage with others.
- <u>Short-term stays at assisted living or memory care facilities</u>: Some facilities offer short-term respite stays, providing a temporary change of scenery and professional care for your loved one. This can be particularly helpful if you need to travel or take an extended break from caregiving.
- <u>Family and friends</u>: Remember to appreciate the power of your existing support network. Reach out to family members or friends willing to provide temporary care or assistance. Even a few hours of respite can significantly affect your overall well-being.

Choosing the right respite care option depends on your loved one's needs, your own preferences, and your budget. Consider factors such as their level of care needs, their comfort with new environments, and the availability of services in your area. It's also important to communicate openly with your loved one about respite care, explaining its benefits and addressing any concerns they may have.

While taking a break from caregiving may initially feel daunting or even guilt-inducing, it's crucial to remember that respite care is not about abandoning your loved one. It's about prioritizing your own health and well-being so you can continue to provide the best possible care. When you're rested, refreshed, and emotionally balanced, you're better equipped to handle caregiving challenges and cherish the moments of joy and connection with your loved one.

Taking breaks can also benefit your loved one. Respite care can provide them with opportunities for social interaction, engagement in new activities, and a change of scenery. It can also allow them to build relationships with other caregivers and individuals with dementia, fostering a sense of community and belonging.

Be sure to seek respite care before you're on the verge of burnout. Incorporate regular breaks into your caregiving routine, even if it's just for a few hours each week. Plan activities you enjoy, connect with friends and family, or take some time for quiet reflection and self-care.

Remember, you're not alone in this journey. Resources and support are available to help you find the respite care options that best meet your needs. Contact your local Area Agency on Aging, Alzheimer's Association chapter, or other community organizations for information and guidance. By prioritizing your own well-being and seeking respite care when needed, you can ensure a more sustainable and fulfilling caregiving experience for both you and your loved one.

The most important thing a caregiver can do is to take care of themselves." – Unknown

CHAPTER 6 PRACTICAL EXERCISE

I want to encourage you to continue with journaling, with even more focus on self-care. Remember, there are no correct answers. Here are some more starting points for your journal, but feel free to use the journal to your best benefit.

1. What activities help you relax and de-stress? Consider physical activities, hobbies, or spending time in nature.
2. How can you give priority to self-care among your caregiving responsibilities? Write down any strategies to use in your busy schedule.
3. Are there any support systems that you can rely on for emotional support? This could include friends, family, support groups, or therapy.
4. Have you found any way to balance your own needs with the needs of your loved one? Remember, self-care is not selfish; it is essential for you to provide the best possible care for your loved one.

7

ADVOCATING FOR CHANGE AND CREATING DEMENTIA-FRIENDLY SOCIETIES

With dementia care, advocacy is a powerful force, a voice that speaks for those whose voices may be silenced by the progression of the disease. It's about standing up for the rights, dignity, and well-being of individuals with dementia, ensuring they receive the care, support, and respect they deserve. It's about raising awareness, challenging stigma, and advocating for policies and practices that create a more inclusive and compassionate society. Alzheimer's Disease International (ADI) provides a comprehensive guide on building such communities, emphasizing the importance of raising awareness, reducing stigma, and promoting inclusivity for individuals with dementia. Alzheimer's Disease International (ADI). (2013). Dementia-friendly Communities.

Advocacy is not just about fighting for change on a grand scale; it's also about making a difference in the lives of individuals and families affected by dementia. It can involve simple acts of kindness, such as speaking up for your loved one's needs at a doctor's appointment or advocating for their inclusion in social activities. It can also involve more formal efforts, such as joining advocacy organizations, contacting elected officials, or taking part in research studies.

One of the most important roles of advocacy is raising awareness about dementia. Many people still hold misconceptions about the disease, viewing it as a normal part of aging or a sign of weakness. By sharing your experiences, educating others, and taking part in public awareness campaigns, you can help dispel these myths and promote a more accurate understanding of dementia.

Challenging stigma is another crucial aspect of advocacy. Individuals with dementia often face discrimination and social isolation, their voices silenced by the fear and misunderstanding that surround the disease. By speaking out against stigma, advocating for inclusive policies, and promoting a more compassionate approach to dementia care, you can help create a society where individuals with dementia are valued, respected, and included.

Advocacy also plays a vital role in shaping policies and practices that affect dementia care. By contacting your elected officials, sharing your experiences, and advocating for increased funding for research, support services, and caregiver resources, you can help create a more dementia-friendly society. Your voice matters, and it can make a real difference in the lives of countless individuals and families.

Participating in research studies is another way to contribute to the fight against dementia. By volunteering your time and sharing your experiences, you can help researchers gain a deeper understanding of the disease, develop new treatments, and ultimately find a cure. Your participation can be a powerful legacy, contributing to a future where dementia is no longer a threat.

Advocacy is not just about speaking out; it's also about listening. Listen to the voices of individuals with dementia, their caregivers, and their families. Understand their needs, their challenges, and their hopes for the future. Use this knowledge to inform your advocacy efforts and create a more compassionate and responsive care system.

Remember, advocacy is not a solo endeavor. It's about building coalitions, collaborating with others, and leveraging collective power to create change. Connect with advocacy organizations, support groups, and others who share your passion for improving the lives of those affected by dementia. Together, you can amplify your voices, create a ripple effect of change, and build a more dementia-friendly world.

Whether through small acts of kindness, public awareness campaigns, or political advocacy, your voice matters. By embracing the role of advocate, you can honor the lives of those living with dementia, empower their caregivers, and contribute to a future where dementia is no longer a source of fear and isolation.

CREATING DEMENTIA-FRIENDLY SPACES: A GUIDE FOR COMMUNITIES

Imagine a world where individuals with dementia can easily navigate their surroundings, where familiar landmarks and clear signage guide their steps, where compassionate faces greet them with understanding, and where opportunities for engagement and connection abound. This vision of a dementia-friendly community is not a distant dream; it's a reality we can create together, one step at a time. By fostering awareness, promoting inclusivity, and making thoughtful adjustments to our physical and social environments, we can transform our communities into havens of support and understanding for those living with dementia and their caregivers.

Creating dementia-friendly spaces is not just about physical modifications; it's about cultivating a culture of compassion where individuals with dementia feel valued, respected, and included. It's about recognizing that they are still active members of our communities with unique needs and abilities that deserve acknowledgment and support. It's about creating an environment where they can thrive, not just survive.

One of the first steps in creating a dementia-friendly community is to promote awareness and understanding of the disease. Educate local businesses, organizations, and community members about the challenges faced by individuals with dementia and their caregivers. Offer training sessions on effective communication strategies, recognizing signs of distress, and providing assistance when needed. By fostering a deeper understanding of dementia, we can reduce stigma, promote empathy, and create a more welcoming and supportive environment.

Physical modifications can also make a significant difference in creating dementia-friendly spaces. Clear signage, contrasting colors, and well-lit pathways can help individuals with dementia navigate their surroundings more easily and confidently. Consider installing handrails, grab bars, and other assistive devices in public spaces to enhance safety and accessibility. Creating quiet spaces where individuals can retreat from sensory overload can also be beneficial.

Transportation can be a significant challenge for individuals with dementia and their caregivers. Advocate for accessible and affordable transportation options, such as specialized transportation services or ride-sharing programs designed for individuals with disabilities. Encourage local businesses and organizations to offer dementia-friendly hours or services, such as early-bird shopping hours or memory cafes where individuals with dementia and their caregivers can socialize and engage in activities.

Social inclusion is crucial for maintaining quality of life and preventing isolation. Encourage community members to reach out to individuals with dementia and their families, offering support, companionship, and opportunities for engagement. Organize intergenerational activities, such as art classes or music programs, that bring together people of all ages and abilities.

Businesses and organizations can also play a vital role in creating dementia-friendly communities. Train staff members on interacting with individuals with dementia, offer dementia-friendly menus or services and create welcoming and inclusive environments. Simple gestures, such as providing a helping hand or a friendly smile, can make a world of difference.

Remember, creating a dementia-friendly community is an ongoing process that requires collaboration, commitment, and a shared vision of inclusivity. It's about recognizing the unique needs of individuals with dementia and their caregivers and working together to create an environment where they feel valued, supported, and empowered. By fostering awareness, promoting understanding, and making thoughtful adjustments to our physical and social spaces, we can build communities that celebrate the lives of those living with dementia and embrace them as integral members of our society.

NAVIGATING PUBLIC SITUATIONS WITH DEMENTIA

Venturing into the public sphere with a loved one living with dementia can be a mix of anticipation and apprehension. Once a familiar and welcoming space, the world outside can suddenly feel filled with challenges and uncertainties. From navigating crowded stores to attending social gatherings, these outings can trigger anxiety, confusion, and even behavioral changes in individuals with dementia. As a caregiver, your role is to create a supportive and empowering environment where your loved one feels safe, respected, and included, even as they navigate the complexities of social interactions.

Preparation is key to a successful outing. Choose destinations and activities that are familiar and enjoyable for your loved one. Consider their interests, abilities, and sensitivities when planning outings. Avoid crowded or noisy environments that might trigger anxiety or confusion. Choose quieter times of the day or less busy locations to minimize sensory overload.

Communicate clearly and patiently. Explain where you are going, what you will do, and who you might encounter. Use simple, direct language and avoid overwhelming your loved one with too much information at once. Be prepared to repeat yourself and offer reassurance if they become confused or anxious.

Be mindful of your loved one's cues. Pay attention to their body language, facial expressions, and verbalizations. Take a break or adjust your plans if they seem overwhelmed or uncomfortable. Remember, their well-being is paramount, and cutting an outing short is okay if needed.

Maintain a sense of humor and flexibility. Things may not always go according to plan, and that's okay. Embrace the unexpected, find humor in the challenges, and be willing to adapt your approach as needed. Remember, it's not about achieving perfection but creating positive experiences and fostering connections.

When interacting with others, be prepared to advocate for your loved one. Explain their condition in a clear and concise manner, and don't hesitate to ask for help or accommodations if needed. Most people are understanding and willing to help, but they may not be aware of the challenges faced by individuals with dementia.

Encourage social interaction and engagement. While dementia can lead to social withdrawal, maintaining social connections is crucial for emotional well-being. Encourage your loved one to take part in conversations, share their thoughts and feelings, and connect with others. Be patient and supportive and create opportunities for meaningful interactions.

Be mindful of potential triggers for agitation or confusion. Large crowds, loud noises, unfamiliar faces, or changes in routine can all contribute to anxiety and behavioral changes. If you notice your loved one becoming overwhelmed, gently guide them to a quieter space or offer reassurance and support.

Remember, every outing is an opportunity for connection, joy, and shared experiences. Focus on the positive moments, celebrate small victories, and cherish the time you spend together. Creating a supportive and empowering environment can help your loved one navigate social situations with confidence and grace.

Navigating public situations with dementia requires patience, understanding, and a willingness to adapt. It's about creating a safe and supportive space where your loved one feels comfortable and respected. By preparing in advance, communicating clearly, and being mindful of their needs, you can create positive and meaningful experiences that enhance their quality of life and foster a sense of belonging.

In the midst of dementia caregiving, where emotions run high, and challenges seem endless, support groups emerge as beacons of hope, offering a safe harbor for those navigating the struggles. They provide a space for connection, understanding, and shared experiences, reminding caregivers that they are not alone in this journey. Within these circles of compassion, individuals find solace, strength, and a renewed sense of purpose.

Support groups are gatherings of individuals who share a common experience, in this case, caring for a loved one with dementia. They offer a safe and confidential space to express feelings, share stories, exchange information, and receive emotional support. Whether it's a formal group facilitated by a professional or a casual gathering of friends and family, these connections can be invaluable for caregivers.

One of the most powerful aspects of support groups is the sense of community they foster. Caregiving can be an isolating experience as you navigate the challenges of the disease and witness the gradual decline of your loved one. Support groups provide a sense of belonging, where you can connect with others who truly understand what you're going through. Sharing your experiences, both the triumphs and the struggles, can be incredibly cathartic and validating. It reminds you that you're not alone and that there are others who share your journey.

Support groups also offer a wealth of information and resources. Members can exchange practical tips on managing challenging behaviors, navigating the healthcare system, and accessing community services. They can also share information about the latest research, treatment options, and caregiver resources. This collective knowledge can empower you to make informed decisions and feel more confident in your caregiving role.

Beyond the practical benefits, support groups provide a much-needed source of emotional support. Caregiving can be an emotional rollercoaster, filled with moments of joy, sadness, anger, and frustration. Support groups offer a safe space to express these emotions without fear of judgment. Sharing your feelings with others who understand can be incredibly therapeutic, helping you process your grief, reduce stress, and find moments of peace and solace.

Support groups can also foster a sense of hope and optimism. Hearing the stories of other caregivers who have successfully navigated the challenges of dementia can inspire you and remind you that there is light at the end of the tunnel. Sharing your own triumphs and successes can also be empowering, reminding you of your own strength and resilience.

If you're looking for a support group in your community, start by contacting local hospitals, senior centers, religious organizations, or the Alzheimer's Association. They often offer a variety of support groups tailored to different needs and stages of the disease. You can also search online for virtual support groups or forums that connect caregivers from all over the world.

If you can't find a support group that meets your needs, consider starting your own. Reach out to other caregivers in your community, connect with them online, or partner with a local organization to create a safe and welcoming space for sharing experiences and offering support.

Remember, building a support network is an essential part of self-care for caregivers. By connecting with others, sharing your experiences, and receiving support, you can navigate the challenges of dementia caregiving with greater ease and grace. You'll find strength in shared experiences, hope in the face of adversity, and a community of compassionate individuals who understand your journey.

EDUCATING OTHERS: RAISING AWARENESS AND UNDERSTANDING

In dementia care, education emerges as a powerful tool, bringing together knowledge, compassion, and a shared vision for a more inclusive and supportive society. As caregivers, we have a unique opportunity to become educators, sharing our experiences, insights, and understanding of dementia with those around us. By raising awareness, challenging misconceptions, and fostering empathy, we can break down the barriers of stigma and create a world where individuals with dementia are valued, and embraced.

Education is the key to unlocking understanding and dispelling the myths that often surround dementia. Many people still view dementia as a normal part of aging, a simple matter of forgetfulness, or even a sign of weakness or incompetence. These misconceptions can lead to fear, discrimination, and social isolation for individuals with dementia and their families. By sharing our knowledge and experiences, we can challenge these stereotypes and promote a more accurate and compassionate understanding of the disease. We can help others see beyond the diagnosis and recognize the personhood, the strengths, and the unique challenges faced by those living with dementia.

Start by educating your own family and friends. Talk openly about your loved one's diagnosis, explain the challenges they face, and share the strategies you've learned for effective communication and care. Encourage them to ask questions, express their concerns, and learn alongside you. By fostering open dialogue and understanding within your own circle, you can create a supportive and empowering environment for your loved one. Sharing your personal journey can help others understand the realities of dementia and dispel any fears or misconceptions they may have.

Extend your reach beyond your immediate circle by engaging with your community. Offer to speak at local schools, churches, or community centers about dementia and the importance of early diagnosis and intervention. Share your story, highlighting the challenges and triumphs of caregiving, and offer practical tips for interacting with individuals with dementia. Sharing your knowledge and experiences can inspire others to become more compassionate and understanding. Your voice can make a real difference in shaping public perception and creating a more inclusive society.

Use social media and other online platforms to raise awareness and connect with other caregivers and advocates. Share articles, blog posts, and personal stories about dementia care. Take part in online discussions and forums, offering support and encouragement to others. By leveraging the power of social media, you can reach a wider audience and amplify your message of compassion and understanding. These platforms provide a powerful way to connect with others, share resources, and create a virtual community of support.

Consider organizing or taking part in local events and fundraisers to support dementia research and advocacy organizations. These events can raise awareness, generate funds for crucial research, and foster a sense of community and shared purpose. By getting involved, you can make a tangible difference in the fight against dementia misinformation and contribute to a future where a cure is possible. Your active participation can inspire others to act and create a ripple effect of change.

Education is not just about imparting information; it's about fostering empathy and understanding. Share stories that humanize dementia, showcasing the unique personalities, strengths, and challenges of individuals living with the disease. Encourage others to see beyond the diagnosis and recognize every person's inherent worth and dignity. By sharing personal anecdotes and experiences, you can help others connect with the emotional reality of dementia and break down the barriers of stigma.

Remember, education is an ongoing process. As you learn more about dementia, share your knowledge with others. Challenge misconceptions, advocate for change, and promote a more inclusive and compassionate society. By educating others, you're not just helping individuals with dementia; you're creating a ripple effect of understanding and support that can transform our communities and pave the way for a brighter future.

Your voice matters. Your experiences matter. By sharing your story and raising awareness about dementia, you can make a profound difference in the lives of countless individuals and families. Together, we can build a world where dementia is no longer a source of fear and isolation but rather an opportunity for compassion, connection, and hope.

LEVERAGING SOCIAL MEDIA FOR SUPPORT AND ADVOCACY

In today's interconnected world, social media has emerged as a powerful platform for connection, communication, and community building. For dementia caregivers, it offers a unique opportunity to find support, share experiences, and advocate for change. By harnessing the reach and influence of social media, we can amplify our voices, create a virtual network of support, and contribute to a more dementia-friendly society.

Social media platforms, such as Facebook, Twitter, Instagram, and TikTok, provide a space for caregivers to connect with others who are navigating similar journeys. By joining online groups and forums dedicated to dementia care, you can access a wealth of information, share your experiences, and receive emotional support from fellow caregivers. These virtual communities can be especially valuable for those living in remote areas or with limited access to in-person support groups.

Sharing your story on social media can be a powerful way to raise awareness about dementia and challenge stigma. By posting personal anecdotes, photos, and videos, you can humanize the disease, showcase the resilience of individuals with dementia, and inspire others to offer compassion and understanding. Your story can resonate with countless others, creating a ripple effect of empathy and support.

Social media also offers a platform for advocacy. By sharing information about dementia research, treatment options, and caregiver resources, you can educate your network and empower others to take action. You can also use social media to advocate for policy changes, raise funds for research, and promote a more dementia-friendly society. Your voice can reach a wider audience and inspire others to join the fight against dementia.

Engage with other caregivers and advocacy organizations on social media. Follow relevant hashtags, participate in online discussions, and share your insights and experiences. You can build relationships, exchange information, and foster a sense of collective action by actively engaging with the online community.

Use social media to celebrate the lives of individuals with dementia. Share their accomplishments, their passions, and their unique personalities. Highlight their contributions to their families and communities and challenge the stereotypes that often surround dementia. By showcasing the resilience and humanity of those living with the disease, you can help break down stigma and promote a more inclusive society.

Be mindful of privacy and ethical considerations when sharing information about your loved one on social media. Always obtain their consent before posting any personal information or images. Respect their dignity and avoid sharing anything that might be embarrassing or seem exploitative.

Remember, social media is a powerful tool that can be used for good. By using it to connect with others, share your story, and advocate for change, you can contribute to a more dementia-friendly world. Your voice matters, and it can make a real difference in the lives of countless individuals and families.

In the digital age, social media offers a unique opportunity to build community, foster understanding, and amplify our voices in the fight against dementia. By leveraging its power, we can create a virtual network of support, educate others, challenge stigma, and advocate for change. Together, we can harness the power of social media to create a more compassionate and inclusive society for individuals with dementia and their caregivers.

You are not alone. Millions of people are walking a similar path. Find them. Connect with them. Share the journey. - Nancy L. Kriseman, author and advocate

Continue with your journaling with a new focus on creating or maintaining a support system. Reflect on the ways that you have found support or where to start going forward.

1. Who is your current support system? Friends, family, or professionals?
2. How do they support you? Emotionally, physically or financially?
3. How has your support system changed over time?
4. Do you have advice for others needing support? Share your insights.

8

FINDING PEACE AND PURPOSE

While caring for a loved one with dementia, the caregiver's role is paved with enormous challenges and unexpected rewards. It's a calling that beckons us to step outside of ourselves, to put the needs of another before our own, and to navigate a path filled with heartache and profound love. While caregiving for a loved one with dementia can be an arduous journey, it can also be a transformative experience, offering opportunities for personal growth, deeper connection, and a profound sense of meaning and purpose.

Embracing the role of caregiver is not about denying the difficulties or minimizing the sacrifices involved. It's about acknowledging the challenges and recognizing the profound privilege of accompanying your loved one on this journey. It's about finding strength in vulnerability, discovering resilience in the face of adversity, and recognizing the transformative power of love.

One of the most profound aspects of caregiving is the opportunity to deepen your connection with your loved one. As dementia progresses, communication may become challenging, and memories may fade, but the essence of your relationship remains. Through simple acts of kindness, shared moments of joy, and unwavering presence, you can create a bond that transcends the limitations of the disease. It's about seeing beyond the cognitive decline and connecting with the heart and soul of the person you love. Even amid confusion and forgetfulness, love can find a way to shine through, creating moments of profound intimacy and understanding.

Caregiving can also be a catalyst for personal growth and self-discovery. As you navigate the complexities of dementia, you may find yourself developing new skills, tapping into hidden strengths, and discovering a resilience you never knew you possessed. You may learn to be more patient, compassionate, and present in the moment. You may also find a newfound appreciation for the simple things in life, the beauty of nature, the power of human connection, and the preciousness of time. The challenges of caregiving can push you beyond your comfort zone, forcing you to confront your own vulnerabilities and emerge stronger on the other side.

Finding meaning and purpose in caregiving can provide profound strength and solace. It's about recognizing the value of your role, the impact you have on your loved one's life, and the legacy you're creating. It's about finding fulfillment in the act of giving, in the selfless devotion that defines the caregiver's journey. Even on the most challenging days, knowing that you are providing comfort, love, and dignity to your loved one can bring a sense of purpose and fulfillment that transcends the challenges.

While caregiving can be isolating, it can also be an opportunity to connect with a broader support community. Reach out to other caregivers, share your experiences, and learn from their wisdom. Join support groups, participate in online forums, and attend educational events. These connections can provide a sense of belonging, validation, and encouragement, reminding you that you're not alone in this journey. Sharing your struggles and triumphs with others who understand can be incredibly therapeutic and empowering.

Remember, embracing the role of caregiver is not about sacrificing your own happiness or well-being. It's about finding a balance between giving and receiving, between caring for your loved one and caring for yourself. Make time for self-care, pursue activities you enjoy, and nurture your own physical, emotional, and spiritual health. By taking care of yourself, you'll be better equipped to care for your loved one and to find joy and fulfillment in the journey.

Embracing the role of caregiver is a courageous act of love that can transform your life in profound ways. It's a journey filled with challenges but also with moments of grace, connection, and deep meaning. By acknowledging the difficulties, celebrating the victories, and prioritizing your own well-being, you can navigate this path with resilience, compassion, and a newfound sense of purpose.

CELEBRATING SMALL VICTORIES AND JOYFUL MOMENTS

In the often-overwhelming experience of dementia caregiving, it's easy to become consumed by the challenges, the losses, and the uncertainties that lie ahead. The gradual loss of cognitive abilities, the unpredictable behaviors, and the constant adjustments to a new reality can leave you feeling drained and discouraged. But there are also moments of light, small victories, and joyful moments that remind us of the enduring power of love, connection, and the human spirit. It's about celebrating these precious moments, however fleeting, and finding solace in the simple joys that dementia cannot steal.

Celebrating small victories is about recognizing and appreciating the accomplishments, however minor they may seem. It's about acknowledging the effort your loved one puts forth to complete a task, even if it's something they once did effortlessly. It's about rejoicing in a moment of clarity, a shared laugh, or a tender embrace. These small victories, like tiny beacons of hope, illuminate the path and remind us that there is still room for joy and celebration, even in the face of adversity.

Perhaps your loved one struggles to remember names or faces, but they surprise you by recalling a cherished memory from their childhood. Or maybe they have difficulty dressing themselves, but they beam with pride when they manage to button their shirt. These seemingly insignificant moments can be a source of immense joy and a reminder of the resilience that lies within.

Joyful moments can also be found in the simplest of shared experiences. A walk in the park, a cup of tea on the porch, or listening to their favorite music together can create a sense of connection and happiness that transcends the challenges of dementia. These moments, where time seems to stand still and the weight of the world fades away, are precious gifts to be treasured.

Humor, too, can be a powerful source of joy and connection. Even as dementia progresses, individuals often retain their sense of humor, enjoying life's absurdities or sharing a laugh over a silly joke. Embrace these lighthearted moments, allowing yourself to laugh and connect with your loved one on a deeper level. Laughter can be a balm for the soul, easing tension, reducing stress, and reminding both of you of the joy still in the world.

It's important to be present and mindful, to actively seek out and appreciate these moments of joy and connection. Put away distractions, turn off the television, and be with your loved one. Listen to their stories, observe their expressions, and engage in activities that bring them pleasure. These moments of shared experience can create lasting memories and foster a sense of love and belonging.

Don't be afraid to express your love and appreciation. Tell your loved one how much you care, admire their strength, and are grateful for the time you have together. These words of affirmation can be compelling, providing comfort, reassurance, and a sense of validation.

Remember, celebrating small victories and joyful moments is not about denying the reality of dementia or minimizing its challenges. It's about finding the light in the shadows, embracing the present moment, and cherishing your precious time with your loved one. By focusing on the positive, you can create a more joyful and fulfilling experience for you and your loved one, even as you navigate the complexities of dementia care.

NAVIGATING GRIEF AND LOSS WITH GRACE

The dementia caregiving journey is bittersweet, filled with a flow of love, loss, and resilience. As the disease progresses, you may find yourself grieving the gradual fading of your loved one's memories, personality, and independence. It's a profound loss, a slow and agonizing goodbye that can leave you feeling heartbroken, exhausted, and adrift in a sea of sadness. But navigating this grief with grace and acceptance is possible, honoring both the journey and the enduring bond you share with your loved one.

Grief, in the context of dementia, is a complex and multifaceted emotion. It's not just about mourning the physical loss of your loved one, but also the loss of their cognitive abilities, their sense of self, and the shared memories that once defined your relationship. It's a grief that can be as deep and profound as any other, and it deserves to be acknowledged, honored, and processed with compassion.

One of the most challenging aspects of grieving in dementia care is the ambiguity of the loss. Unlike other forms of grief, where there's a clear endpoint, dementia is a slow and gradual decline. You may find yourself mourning the loss of your loved one's abilities and personality long before they physically pass away. This can lead to a sense of anticipatory grief, where you're constantly grieving the losses that have already occurred and those that are yet to come. It's a grief that ebbs and flows, sometimes overwhelming, sometimes subtle, but always present.

It's also common to experience a sense of disenfranchised grief, where your feelings of loss are not fully acknowledged or validated by others. Society often views dementia as a natural part of aging, minimizing the profound impact it has on individuals and their families. This can leave caregivers feeling isolated and misunderstood, adding another layer of complexity to their grief.

Navigating this grief requires patience, self-compassion, and a willingness to seek support. There's no right or wrong way to grieve, and what works for one person may not work for another. However, there are strategies that can help you cope with the emotional challenges and find moments of peace and solace amidst the storm.

Allow yourself to feel your emotions without judgment. Don't suppress your grief or pretend that everything is okay. Instead, acknowledge your feelings, express them in healthy ways, and give yourself time to heal. Whether through journaling, talking to a trusted friend or therapist, or simply allowing yourself to cry, processing these emotions is essential to the healing process.

Connect with others who understand what you're going through. Consider joining a support group for dementia caregivers, where you can share your experiences, receive validation, and learn from others who are navigating a similar journey. Talking to a therapist or counselor can also provide a safe space to process your grief and develop coping mechanisms. Remember, you're not alone in this.

Find ways to honor your loved one's life and legacy. Create a memory book or scrapbook filled with photos and stories. Share their favorite music or movies. Continue traditions that were important to them. These acts of remembrance can help you stay connected to your loved one, even as their memories fade. They can also provide a sense of comfort and continuity, reminding you of the beautiful life they lived and the impact they had on the world.

Practice self-care. Grief can be physically and emotionally exhausting. Make sure you're getting enough sleep, eating nutritious meals, and exercising regularly. Engage in activities you enjoy, spend time with loved ones, and seek moments of peace and solitude. Taking care of yourself is not selfish; it's essential for your own well-being and your ability to continue providing compassionate care.

Remember, grief is a journey, not a destination. It's a process that unfolds over time, with its unique twists and turns. Be patient with yourself, allow yourself to feel your emotions, and seek support when needed. By navigating this grief with grace and acceptance, you can honor the journey, cherish the memories, and find moments of peace and beauty even in loss.

PLANNING FOR YOUR OWN FUTURE AND WELL-BEING: BEYOND CAREGIVING

While the present moment demands your focus and energy as a caregiver, it's equally crucial to cast your gaze toward the horizon and consider your own future and well-being. The journey of dementia caregiving, while deeply meaningful, can also be all-consuming, leaving little room for personal aspirations, dreams, and plans. However, nurturing your own future is not a selfish act; it's an essential part of ensuring your long-term health, happiness, and resilience.

As the primary caregiver for your loved one with dementia, your days may revolve around their needs, their schedules, and their well-being. It's easy to put your own life on hold, postponing personal goals, neglecting hobbies, and sacrificing your own dreams in service of their care. While this selflessness is admirable, it's also unsustainable in the long run. To continue providing compassionate and effective care, you must also nurture your own future and well-being.

Start by reflecting on your own aspirations and dreams. What are your passions, interests, and goals for the future? What brings you joy, fulfillment, and a sense of purpose? While caregiving may currently occupy a significant portion of your life, it's essential to carve out space for your own dreams and aspirations, however small they may seem.

Consider your financial future. Caregiving can significantly impact your finances, particularly if you've had to reduce your work hours or leave your job altogether. Explore options for financial assistance, such as long-term care insurance, government programs, or non-profit organizations that offer support for caregivers. Consult with a financial advisor to create a plan to ensure your financial security during the caregiving journey and beyond.

Think about your social connections and support network. Caregiving can be isolating, as you may have less time and energy for social activities and relationships. Make a conscious effort to maintain connections with friends and family, even just a quick phone call or a brief visit. Consider joining a support group or online community for caregivers, where you can connect with others who understand your challenges and offer encouragement.

Explore opportunities for personal growth and development. Caregiving can be a time of immense learning and personal transformation. Consider taking classes, pursuing hobbies, or volunteering for causes you care about. These activities can provide a sense of purpose, expand your horizons, and contribute to your overall well-being.

Plan for the future, both during and after your caregiving journey. Think about what you want your life to look like once your caregiving responsibilities have ended. Do you want to return to work, pursue a new career, or dedicate more time to personal interests? Start exploring these possibilities now, setting goals, and taking small steps towards achieving them.

Remember, planning for your own future is not selfish; it's an act of self-preservation and empowerment. By nurturing your own dreams, aspirations, and well-being, you're not only ensuring your own happiness but also creating a sustainable and fulfilling caregiving experience. When you're emotionally and physically healthy, you're better equipped to provide compassionate and effective care for your loved one.

As you navigate the complexities of dementia caregiving, don't lose sight of your own future. Embrace the opportunities for growth, connection, and self-discovery this journey offers. Plan for your financial security, nurture your social connections, and prioritize your own well-being. By doing so, you'll not only honor the life of your loved one but also create a brighter and more fulfilling future for yourself.

CULTIVATING HOPE AND RESILIENCE FOR THE ROAD AHEAD

In the challenging process of dementia caregiving, hope and resilience become guiding lights, illuminating the path even in the darkest of times. They are the seeds we plant within ourselves, nurtured by love, compassion, and a deep belief in the enduring power of the human spirit. As caregivers, we must cultivate these seeds, tending to them with care and allowing them to grow into strength and renewal.

Hope is not a naïve optimism that ignores the realities of dementia. It's a steadfast belief in the possibility of finding meaning, connection, and joy even amidst the challenges. It's a recognition that even as cognitive abilities decline, the essence of our loved one remains. Their spirits are still capable of experiencing love, laughter, and moments of profound connection. Hope is the fuel that keeps us going, the light that guides us through the darkness.

Resilience is the ability to bend without breaking, to adapt to the ever-changing landscape of dementia, and to emerge from the depths of despair with renewed strength and determination. It's about cultivating a mindset that embraces challenges as opportunities for growth, recognizing your own strengths and limitations, and finding meaning and purpose in adversity. It's about learning to navigate the emotional rollercoaster of caregiving, to find moments of peace and joy even in the face of loss, and to emerge from the experience with a deeper sense of compassion and understanding.

Cultivating hope and resilience requires a conscious effort, a commitment to nurturing your own well-being, and finding strength in the face of adversity. It's about recognizing that you are not alone in this journey and that countless resources and support systems are available to help you along the way.

One way to cultivate hope is to focus on the present moment. Dementia can rob us of the past and the future, but it can't take away the here and now. Cherish your time with your loved one, create fresh memories, and celebrate the moments of connection and joy. Even in the later stages of the disease, there are still opportunities for meaningful interactions and shared experiences. These moments, however fleeting, are precious gifts to be treasured.

Another way to foster resilience is to practice gratitude. Even amid challenges, there are always things to be grateful for. Take time each day to reflect on the blessings in your life, the love you share with your loved one, the support of family and friends, and the small victories that bring you joy. Gratitude can shift your perspective, reminding you of the abundance that surrounds you, even in the face of adversity.

Self-care is also essential for developing hope and resilience. Make time for activities you enjoy, connect with friends and family, and prioritize your own physical and emotional health. By taking care of yourself, you'll be better equipped to handle the challenges of caregiving and maintain a positive outlook. Remember, you can't pour from an empty cup.

Finally, feel free to seek professional help if needed. Therapists, counselors, and support groups can provide valuable guidance and coping strategies for navigating the emotional complexities of caregiving. Talking to someone who understands can help you process your feelings, reduce stress, and find renewed strength and hope.

The road ahead may be long and winding, but by through hope and resilience, you can navigate it with grace and courage.

Remember, you are not alone. Countless others have walked this path before you; their stories of strength and perseverance can inspire you. By nurturing the seeds of hope and resilience within yourself, you can create a more positive and empowering experience for both you and your loved one, even as you face the challenges of dementia together.

THE HEALING POWER OF SHARING YOUR STORY

The simple act of sharing your story can be a powerful source of healing, connection, and empowerment. It's about breaking the silence, shedding light on the hidden struggles and triumphs of caregiving, and finding solace in the shared experiences of others. It's about recognizing that your voice matters, your story has value, and by speaking your truth, you can heal yourself and inspire and uplift others who are walking a similar path.

Sharing your story is not about boasting or seeking pity; it's about connecting with others on a human level, fostering empathy, and building a support community. It's about acknowledging the raw emotions, the difficult decisions, and the moments of grace that shape the caregiving experience. It's about giving voice to the unspoken, shedding light on the often-invisible struggles of caregivers, and reminding the world that dementia is not just a medical diagnosis but a profoundly personal journey.

There are countless ways to share your story. You can write a blog or journal, participate in online forums and support groups, or even speak at community events or conferences. You can share your experiences with friends and family, creating a safe space for open dialogue and understanding. You can also contribute to research studies or advocacy efforts, using your voice to shape policies and practices that affect dementia care.

The act of sharing your story can be incredibly cathartic. It allows you to process your emotions, make sense of your experiences, and find meaning amid chaos. Writing or speaking about your journey can help you gain perspective, identify patterns, and discover hidden strengths and resilience within yourself. It can also be a way to honor your loved one, celebrating their life and legacy while acknowledging the challenges of dementia.

Sharing your story can also have a profound impact on others. It can inspire other caregivers, offering them hope, encouragement, and practical advice. It can educate the public about dementia, challenging stereotypes and promoting a more compassionate and inclusive society. It can even influence policymakers and researchers, highlighting the urgent need for increased funding and support for dementia care.

By sharing your story, you're not just telling your own experience but contributing to a collective narrative of resilience, love, and hope. You're creating a ripple effect of understanding and empathy that can extend far beyond your immediate circle.

Of course, sharing your story is a personal choice, and it's essential to do so in a way that feels safe and comfortable for you. You can remain anonymous, share only certain aspects of your experience, or focus on the positive aspects of caregiving. The key is to find a way to express yourself authentically and to connect with others who can offer support and understanding.

Remember, your story matters. Your voice is powerful. By sharing your experiences, you can contribute to a more compassionate and informed society, one that embraces and supports individuals with dementia and their caregivers. You can inspire others, foster hope, and create a legacy of love and resilience that will endure long after the final chapter of your caregiving journey.

And in the end, it's not the years in your life that count. It's the life in your years. - Abraham Lincoln

CHAPTER 8 PRACTICAL EXERCISE

Continue with your journaling with a new focus on creating lasting memories. Reflect on the activities that your loved one enjoys and jot them down for later use to calm those tense situations.

1. What activities bring joy to the both of you? Describe the activity and explain why you both enjoy them.
2. What have you learned about your loved one's preferences and their personality? Have they deepened your connection?
3. How do these shared experiences impact your relationship? Describe any emotional benefits of spending quality time together.

9

STORIES OF HOPE, LOVE, AND FULFILLMENT

In the heart of dementia, where memories fade and the familiar world dissolves into fragments, love remains a steadfast beacon, illuminating the path and guiding us through the darkness. It's a love that transcends the boundaries of cognition, a deep and enduring connection that defies the ravages of the disease. In this chapter, we delve into the heart-warming stories of individuals who have found ways to nurture and express love in the face of dementia, offering a glimpse into the human spirit's resilience and the heart's enduring power.

These stories are not fairy tales but real-life accounts of ordinary people facing extraordinary challenges. They are stories of spouses, children, siblings, and friends who have chosen to walk alongside their loved ones on this journey, offering unwavering support, compassion, and unconditional love. They are stories of resilience, creativity, and the steadfast belief that love can conquer even the most formidable obstacles.

One such story is that of Maria and Carlos, a couple married for over 50 years. When Carlos was diagnosed with Alzheimer's disease, Maria was devastated. She watched as her once-vibrant husband slowly retreated into a world of confusion and forget-fulness. But Maria refused to give up. She learned everything she could about dementia, adapted their home to create a safe and supportive environment, and found creative ways to connect with Carlos, even as his memories faded.

One day, while looking through old photographs, Maria stumbled upon a picture of their wedding day. She showed it to Carlos, and his eyes lit up with recognition. He reached out and gently touched her face, a smile spreading across his lips. At that moment, Maria knew that their love, though challenged by dementia, was still alive and strong.

Another inspiring story is that of Sarah and her mother, Emily. A former pianist, Emily had always found solace and joy in music. As her dementia progressed, she struggled to remember the names of her children and grandchildren, but she could still play the piano beautifully. Sarah often sat beside her mother, listening to her play and singing along to the familiar melodies. Music became their language, a bridge that connected them across the chasm of memory loss.

Then there's the story of David and his father, Robert. Robert, a retired engineer, had always been a man of few words. As his dementia worsened, his communication became even more limited. David, however, discovered a way to connect with his father through their shared love of nature. They would spend hours walking in the park, Robert pointing out birds and trees, his face lighting up with childlike wonder. In these quiet moments, surrounded by the beauty of nature, David felt a profound sense of connection with his father, a connection that transcended words.

These stories, and countless others like them, remind us that dementia does not extinguish love. It may take on new forms and require adaptation and creativity, but it endures. It's in the gentle touch, the shared laughter, the quiet moments of connection that transcend words. It's in the unwavering commitment to care, the selfless acts of devotion, and the enduring bond that defies the ravages of the disease.

Love in the time of dementia is not about grand gestures or extravagant displays of affection. It's about the everyday moments, the simple acts of kindness, and the unwavering presence that speaks volumes. It's about finding new ways to connect, communicate, and express love, even when words fail.

These stories of hope remind us that love can blossom and thrive even in the face of adversity. They inspire us to embrace the challenges of dementia caregiving with courage, compassion, and an unwavering belief in the enduring power of the human spirit. They remind us that love is not a memory; it's a feeling that transcends time and space, a gift that can be given and received, even in the twilight of life.

LESSONS LEARNED FROM CAREGIVING: CAREGIVERS SHARE THEIR INSIGHTS

Dementia caregiving is a profound teacher, offering lessons that extend far beyond the realm of medical knowledge and practical skills. It's a transformative experience that shapes our perspectives, deepens our understanding of love and loss, and reveals the resilience of the human spirit. In this chapter, we delve into the wisdom gleaned from caregivers who have walked this path, sharing their insights, reflections, and hard-earned lessons. These voices, echoing with empathy and understanding, offer a beacon of light to those navigating the complexities of dementia care.

One of the most profound lessons learned from caregiving is the importance of patience. As Mary, a caregiver for her husband with Alzheimer's, shares, "Dementia can be a frustrating and unpredictable disease, and it's easy to become impatient when faced with repetitive questions or challenging behaviors. But I've learned that patience is not just a virtue; it's a necessity. It's about understanding that my husband is not intentionally trying to be difficult; he's simply struggling to cope with the changes in his brain."

Flexibility is another key lesson. Dementia is a progressive disease, and your loved one's needs and abilities will change over time. "What worked yesterday may not work today," says John, who cares for his mother with vascular dementia. "I've had to learn to be flexible, to adapt my approach, and to let go of the need for control. It's about meeting my mom where she is, not where I want her to be."

Compassion is at the heart of dementia caregiving. It's about seeing beyond the disease, recognizing the personhood of your loved one, and treating them with dignity and respect. "Even though my dad's memory is fading," shares Lisa, "he's still the same loving and kind man he's always been. I try to focus on his strengths and abilities and to show him compassion and understanding, even when he's having a difficult day."

Humor, too, can be a powerful tool in navigating the dementia journey. "Sometimes, you just have to laugh," says Tom, who cares for his wife with Lewy body dementia. "There are moments of absurdity and confusion that can be overwhelming, but finding the humor in those situations can help lighten the mood and bring us closer together."

Self-care is another crucial lesson learned by caregivers. "It's easy to neglect your own needs when you're so focused on caring for someone else," admits Karen, a caregiver for her grandmother. "But I've learned that self-care is not selfish; it's essential. I make sure to take breaks, exercise, and connect with friends. It helps me stay grounded and gives me the energy I need to continue providing the best possible care."

Finally, caregivers learn the importance of living in the present moment. "Dementia can rob us of the past and the future," reflects David, who cares for his partner with frontotemporal dementia. "But it can't take away the here and now. I try to cherish every moment with my partner, to focus on the love we share, and to create new memories, even as the old ones fade."

The lessons learned from caregiving are not just about managing a disease but about living a more compassionate, resilient, and fulfilling life. By embracing these lessons, you can provide the best possible care for your loved one and grow as an individual, finding strength, purpose, and a deeper appreciation for the preciousness of life.

THE JOYS AMIDST THE CHALLENGES: FINDING MOMENTS OF HAPPINESS

In the heart of dementia, where shadows of confusion and loss often loom large, a surprising truth exists. Joy can still blossom, even in the most unexpected moments. It's a testament to the enduring human spirit, the resilience of love, and the ability to find beauty and connection even in the face of adversity. As caregivers, we must learn to seek and cherish these joyful moments, for they are the precious gems illuminating the path and reminding us of the profound love and resilience that bind us to our loved ones.

Finding joy amidst the challenges of dementia caregiving is not about denying the difficulties or minimizing the impact of the disease. It's about recognizing that even during cognitive decline, there is still room for laughter, connection, and shared experiences that bring happiness and fulfillment. It's about shifting our focus from what has been lost to what remains and celebrating the moments of grace, humor, and love that emerge along the way.

One of the most profound sources of joy in dementia care is the enduring power of love. Even as memories fade and communication becomes challenging, the deep bond between you and your loved one remains. The gentle touch, the shared smile, and the quiet moments of companionship transcend words. It's in the unwavering devotion, the selfless acts of care, and the unspoken understanding that binds you together. These moments of connection, however fleeting, are a testament to the enduring power of love and the resilience of the human spirit.

Humor, too, can be a powerful source of joy in the dementia journey. Even as cognitive abilities decline, individuals often retain their sense of humor, enjoying life's absurdities or sharing a laugh over a silly joke. Embrace these lighthearted moments, allowing yourself to laugh and connect with your loved one on a deeper level. Laughter can be a balm for the soul, easing tension, reducing stress, and reminding you both of the joy that still exists in the world.

Simple pleasures can also bring immense happiness. A walk in the park, listening to a favorite song, or enjoying a delicious meal together can create moments of shared joy and connection. These experiences, rooted in the senses and emotions, can transcend the limitations of memory and cognition, reminding your loved one of the beauty and wonder that still surrounds them.

Reminiscing can also be a source of joy and connection. Sharing stories, looking at old photographs, or revisiting familiar places can evoke positive emotions and spark memories. Even if your loved one struggles to recall specific details, the emotions and feelings associated with these memories can still be deeply felt.

These shared moments of nostalgia can create a sense of intimacy and belonging, reminding you both of your shared history.

Celebrating milestones and achievements, no matter how small, can also bring a sense of joy and accomplishment. Whether mastering a new skill, completing a puzzle, or simply enjoying a good night's sleep, these victories deserve to be acknowledged and celebrated. They are a testament to your loved one's resilience and ability to adapt and thrive in adversity.

Finally, remember that joy can be found in the most unexpected places. A spontaneous hug, a shared smile, or a moment of quiet companionship can bring a sense of peace and happiness that transcends the challenges of dementia. Be open to these moments, embrace them with gratitude, and allow them to fill your heart with love and hope.

Finding joy amidst the challenges of dementia caregiving is a testament to the enduring power of love, the resilience of the human spirit, and the beauty that can be found even in the most challenging circumstances. By celebrating small victories, cherishing shared moments, and focusing on the positive, we can create a more joyful and fulfilling experience for both ourselves and our loved ones, even as we navigate the complexities of dementia.

EMBRACING CHANGE AND GROWTH THROUGH CAREGIVING: A JOURNEY OF TRANSFORMATION

Dementia caregiving is not just about caring for another; it's also a profound journey of self-discovery and transformation. As we navigate the complexities of this disease, we are inevitably confronted with change, loss, and the impermanence of life. But within these challenges lies an opportunity for growth, a chance to deepen our compassion, cultivate resilience, and emerge from the experience with a newfound appreciation for the preciousness of life.

Embracing change is a fundamental aspect of dementia caregiving. As your loved one's cognitive abilities decline, their personality and behavior may shift, their needs may evolve, and the dynamics of your relationship may transform. It's a constant process of adaptation, requiring flexibility, acceptance, and a willingness to let go of expectations. The person you once knew may gradually become someone different, and it's essential to embrace this new reality, however challenging it may be.

Change can be unsettling, even frightening, but it can also be an opportunity for growth. By embracing the changes in your loved one, you open yourself up to new ways of connecting, communicating, and expressing love. You learn to appreciate the present moment, to find joy in the simple things, and to cherish the time you have together, however fleeting it may be. You may discover hidden reserves of patience, compassion, and creativity as you adapt to the ever-changing landscape of dementia.

Loss is an inevitable part of the dementia journey. You may grieve the loss of your loved one's memories, their independence, their ability to communicate, or even their recognition of you. This grief can be overwhelming, but it's also a testament to the depth of your love and the profound impact your loved one has had on your life. Allow yourself to feel your grief, to express your emotions, and to seek support from others. Remember, grief is a natural part of the healing process, and it's okay not to be okay.

Amidst the challenges of change and loss, there are also growth opportunities. Caregiving can teach you valuable lessons about patience, compassion, and resilience. It can deepen your understanding of the human spirit, its capacity for love, and its ability to find strength in the face of adversity. It can also foster a sense of purpose and meaning as you dedicate yourself to caring for someone you love. The challenges you face can shape you into a stronger, more compassionate, and more resilient individual.

As you navigate this journey, be open to the possibility of transformation. Allow yourself to be changed by the experience, to learn from the challenges, and to embrace the unexpected gifts that may arise. You may discover hidden strengths, develop new skills, or find a renewed appreciation for the simple joys of life. You may also find yourself connecting with your loved one on a deeper level as you learn to communicate through touch, music, and shared moments of presence.

Caregiving can also be a catalyst for personal growth and self-discovery. As you step outside of your comfort zone and face the complexities of dementia, you may find yourself developing new coping mechanisms, strengthening your emotional resilience, and deepening your spiritual connection. You may also discover a newfound sense of purpose and meaning as you dedicate yourself to caring for someone you love. The challenges of caregiving can push you beyond your limits, forcing you to confront your own vulnerabilities and emerge stronger on the other side.

Embrace the journey with all its twists and turns. Allow yourself to be vulnerable, to feel your emotions, and to seek support when needed. Remember, you're not alone in this. Countless others have walked this path before you; their stories of strength and perseverance can inspire you.

By embracing change and growth, you can transform the challenges of dementia caregiving into opportunities for personal and spiritual development. You can emerge from this experience with a deeper sense of compassion, gratitude, and love, a testament to the enduring power of the human spirit. And in the process, you may discover a strength and resilience within yourself that you never knew existed.

PROMISING BREAKTHROUGHS IN DIAGNOSIS, TREATMENT, AND PREVENTION: A BEACON OF HOPE

While dementia remains a formidable challenge, its diagnosis, treatment, and prevention is constantly evolving, offering a glimmer of hope for individuals and families affected by this disease. Scientists and researchers across the globe are tirelessly working to unravel the mysteries of dementia, exploring new avenues for early detection, innovative therapies, and potential preventive measures. In this chapter, we delve into some of the most promising breakthroughs on the horizon, shedding light on the advancements that may one day transform how we understand and manage dementia.

Early diagnosis and intervention are crucial for maximizing quality of life and potentially slowing the progression of dementia. Researchers are developing new diagnostic tools, such as blood tests and brain imaging techniques, to detect the earliest signs of cognitive decline, even before symptoms become apparent. These advancements could lead to earlier interventions, allowing individuals to benefit from treatment and lifestyle modifications at a stage when they can have the most significant impact.

In the realm of treatment, scientists are exploring various innovative approaches. Immunotherapy, which harnesses the power of the immune system to target and clear harmful proteins in the brain, shows promise in slowing or even halting the progression of Alzheimer's disease. Gene therapy, which involves modifying or replacing faulty genes, is another area of active research with the potential to address the underlying causes of certain types of dementia. Stem cell therapy, which uses the regenerative potential of stem cells to repair damaged brain tissue, is also being investigated as a potential treatment option.

Lifestyle modifications are increasingly recognized as powerful tools for both preventing and managing dementia. Research suggests that a healthy diet, regular exercise, social engagement, and cognitive stimulation can all play a role in maintaining brain health and reducing the risk of cognitive decline. Studies have shown that adopting a Mediterranean-style diet, rich in fruits, vegetables, whole grains, and healthy fats, can lower the risk of developing dementia. Regular physical activity, even moderate exercise like walking or gardening, has been linked to improved cognitive function and a reduced risk of Alzheimer's disease.

Social engagement and cognitive stimulation are also crucial for brain health. Staying connected with friends and family, taking part in social activities, and engaging in mentally stimulating pursuits, such as reading, puzzles, or learning new skills, can all help maintain cognitive function and delay the onset of dementia.

Prevention is another area of intense research. Scientists are investigating various risk factors for dementia, including cardiovascular health, diabetes, obesity, and lifestyle choices. By identifying and addressing these risk factors, we may be able to reduce the incidence of dementia and delay its onset. Public health campaigns promoting healthy lifestyle choices and raising awareness about brain health's importance are also crucial in the fight against dementia.

While these promising breakthroughs offer a glimmer of hope, it's important to remember that dementia remains a complex and challenging disease. There's still much we need to learn, and the road to a cure will likely be long and winding. However, the progress being made in research and treatment is encouraging, and it offers a beacon of hope for individuals and families affected by dementia.

As caregivers, it's essential to stay informed about the latest advancements in dementia care. Talk to your loved one's health-care team about new treatment options, participate in research studies if eligible, and advocate for increased funding and support for dementia research. By staying engaged and informed, you can be a part of the solution and contribute to a future where dementia is no longer a devastating diagnosis.

The journey of dementia caregiving is not easy, but it's filled with love, resilience, and the enduring power of the human spirit. By embracing the challenges, celebrating the victories, and looking toward the future with hope, we can create a more compassionate and supportive world for individuals with dementia and their caregivers. And as research continues to advance, we can hold onto the hope that one day, a cure will be found, and dementia will no longer cast its shadow over our lives.

MOVING FORWARD: CARRYING THE LEGACY OF LOVE

Along the path of dementia caregiving, while marked by profound challenges and heartaches, is also a story of deep love, resilience, and growth. As we near the conclusion of this book, it's time to reflect on the lessons learned, the memories cherished, and the legacy of love that remains long after the physical presence of our loved ones has faded.

Moving forward after the loss of a loved one to dementia is a bittersweet experience. It's a time of mourning, of coming to terms with the finality of their passing, and of navigating the complex emotions that accompany grief. But it's also a time of reflection, celebrating a well-lived life, and carrying forward the lessons and love that shaped your experience.

Grief is a natural and necessary part of the healing process. Allow yourself to feel the full spectrum of emotions, from sadness and anger to acceptance and gratitude. Don't suppress your feelings or try to rush through the grieving process. Each person grieves in their own way, and there's no right or wrong timeline. Seek support from family, friends, or a therapist if needed, and allow yourself the time and space to heal. Remember, grief is not a sign of weakness but a testament to the depth of your love.

As you move forward, remember the lessons you learned along the way. The patience, compassion, and resilience you cultivated during your caregiving experience are valuable qualities that will continue to serve you well in all aspects of your life. The deep connection you forged with your loved one, the shared moments of joy and laughter, and the unwavering love that sustained you through the challenges will forever remain a part of you. These lessons, etched in your heart, will shape your interactions with others, deepen your empathy, and enrich your life in countless ways.

Carry forward the legacy of love that your loved one leaves behind. Share their stories, celebrate their accomplishments, and honor their memory in meaningful ways. You might consider volunteering your time to support dementia research or advocacy organizations or simply reaching out to other caregivers to offer support and encouragement. Sharing your experiences and spreading awareness can help create a more compassionate and understanding world for those affected by dementia. Your loved one's life, spirit, and love can continue to inspire and guide you, even in their absence.

As you embark on this new chapter of your life, remember that you are not alone. The bonds you forged with your loved one, the lessons you learned, and the love you shared will forever remain a part of you. Embrace the memories, cherish the moments of joy, and allow the legacy of love to guide you forward. You are stronger than you know, and you have the power to create a meaningful and fulfilling life, even after the challenges of caregiving.

Moving forward doesn't mean forgetting. It's about honoring the past while embracing the future. It's about finding new ways to connect with your loved one, even in their absence. It's about carrying their spirit within you, allowing their love to inspire and guide you on your own path of healing and growth.

As you navigate the path ahead, remember that you are strong, resilient, and capable of creating a meaningful and fulfilling life. Embrace the lessons you've learned, cherish the memories you've made, and allow the legacy of love to illuminate your path. And as you move forward, may you find peace, joy, and a renewed sense of purpose in the world.

I think the best thing I ever did with my life was stand up and say I've got Alzheimer's. - Terry Pratchett

AFTERWORD

As I look back on my experience in caring for my mother through dementia, I am filled with a great sense of gratitude for the lessons learned, the love shared, and the resilience discovered. It was a path fraught with challenges, heartaches, and moments of profound sadness, but it was also a path illuminated by moments of grace, laughter, and enduring love.

This book has been a labor of love, a tribute to my mother and to all the caregivers who navigate the complexities of dementia with unwavering devotion. It's a testament to the enduring power of the human spirit, the resilience of the heart, and the transformative nature of caregiving.

Throughout these chapters, we've explored the many facets of dementia, from its various types and symptoms to its profound impact on individuals and their families. We've delved into the science behind the disease, the emotional rollercoaster of diagnosis and acceptance, and the practical strategies for managing daily care and behavioral changes. We've also explored the importance of self-care, the power of community, and the enduring legacy of love.

But beyond the information and advice, I hope this book has also conveyed a sense of hope, empathy, and understanding. Dementia may be a formidable adversary, but it doesn't have to define us or our loved ones. Despite cognitive decline, there is still room for joy, connection, and meaningful experiences. By embracing the challenges, celebrating the victories, and focusing on the today, we can create a more positive, empowering experience for everyone involved.

As you continue your own caregiving journey, remember that you are not alone. There are countless resources available to support you, from support groups and online communities to healthcare professionals and advocacy organizations. Don't hesitate to reach out for help when you need it and remember to prioritize your own well-being. Self-care is not selfish; it's essential for sustainable and compassionate caregiving.

I encourage you to continue learning about dementia, to advocate for your loved one, and to share your experiences with others. Your voice matters, and it can help in the lives of countless individuals and families.

As we come to the end of this book, let us remember that dementia caregiving, or any caregiving, while challenging, is also a profound opportunity for growth, connection, and love. It's a chance to deepen our understanding of the human spirit, cultivate compassion and resilience, and create a legacy of love that will remain long after our loved ones are gone.

May this book serve as a companion on your journey, offering guidance, support, and a reminder that even in the face of adversity, there is always hope to be found. May it inspire you to embrace the challenges with courage, celebrate the joys with gratitude, and cherish every precious moment with your loved one.

And as you move forward, may you find strength in the love you share, resilience in the face of adversity, and a renewed sense of purpose in the world.

Sometimes the smallest things take up the most room in your heart. - Winnie the Pooh

GLOSSARY

<u>ADLs (Activities of Daily Living)</u>: Basic essential tasks that need to be fulfilled to maintain one's basic needs, such as eating, bathing, toileting, dressing, grooming, and transferring.

<u>Advance Directive (AD)</u>: Document in which the dementia patient explains their wishes and directs how their medical treatment should function. The AD is written and signed while the person is still in possession of their mental faculties.

<u>Agnosia</u>: When the dementia patient fails to recognize people and things through the use of their five senses.

<u>Alzheimer's Disease</u>: The most common cause of dementia in the US, Alzheimer's is a progressive disease that affects memory, thinking, and behavior. Alzheimer's development is often slow, and with time can make common daily tasks impossible.

<u>Anomia</u>: A difficulty to remember how objects are called, which can evolve to mixing the names of things with similar features.

<u>Anosognosia</u>: When one is incapable of understanding that they are physically or neurological impaired.

Apathy: Absence of interest, enthusiasm, or concern.

Appropriate care: The type of care that's selected among all existing types as the one that can offer the most benefit to a specific dementia patient.

Apraxia: Becoming unable to perform complex, learned, familiar, and purposeful movements. People with apraxia may also forget the order of common objects, causing behaviors such as putting a tie under a shirt.

Assessment: The ongoing process of evaluating the person's capacity of living independently and how much help they require.

Automatic thinking scripts: The capacity of completing routine tasks automatically. We all fulfill these scripts without rationalizing each step, which is acquired by repetition. This ability isn't lost with dementia, and the person can fulfill these tasks as long as they're in the same setting and there's no interruption.

Behavioral and Psychological Symptoms of Dementia (BPSD): Disruptive actions from the dementia patient caused by an unmet need. They can manifest as aggressions, compulsions, paranoia, and other unwanted behaviors.

Care Plan: An outline detailing the care goals for people with dementia, by analyzing their physical and psychosocial strengths and weaknesses. This document needs to be developed together with the patients, their families, and any medical specialist that's taking care of the case.

Challenging Behavior: Harsh behavior from the dementia patient, which has the potential of harm or disturb those around them, especially their family and caregivers. This behavior may be born from the frustration of the dementia patient to communicate with those around them.

Creutzfeldt Jacob Disease (CJD): An extremely rare condition caused by the alteration of body proteins by rogue prions, which affects the brain and nervous system.

Cognition: The ensemble of the perceptions that allow us to rationalize and understand ourselves and the world around us.

Cueing: Verbal or visual hints that communicate with the person of dementia so they can start or complete a task. It could be a sentence that makes them turn out the TV and go to bed, or having their outfit laid down in front of them as a cue that they should get dressed.

Delusion: A fixation that an illogical and false situation is true. Delusions often occur when the person mixes and distorts things that actually happen.

Dementia: A term that encompasses several symptoms connected with the loss of memory and cognition, which can be caused by a disease such Alzheimer's, or by a physical injury to the brain.

Depression: An unnatural feeling of sadness and hopelessness that's different from normal daily changes of mood. Depression happens with no apparent reason, though it can be increased by stress, abuse, drug and alcohol abuse, or the loss of a loved one.

Dysarthria: Difficulty to form words and sentences caused by the weakening of the speech muscles.

Dysphagia: Difficulty in swallowing.

Dysphasia: Difficulty in understanding what others say.

Electroencephalography (EEG): Medical test that measures electrical activity in the brain.

Experiential self: The part of our consciousness that is aware of the world around us, and absorbs its stimuli through our five physical senses.

Fight-or-flight response: An acute state of mind that happens when we're in a scary situation. The brain will then release hormones that will allow you to confront that situation or run away until you find a safe place.

Frontal Lobe: The part of the brain behind the forehead that controls emotions, personality, and cognition.

Frontotemporal dementia: A rare type of dementia that affects the frontal lobe of people between their thirties and sixties, affecting their social behavior and capacity of speech. People with frontotemporal dementia are often agitated and incur obsessive and repetitive behavior, but their memory isn't affected during the first stages of the disease.

Gait: An individual's personal walking pattern, which can be affected by dementia to the point of making the person disabled.

Habilitative care: A type of care in which the patient's abilities and disabilities are taken into account, and the environment around is changed in accordance. This helps the patient to retain some autonomy, and be able to fulfill their daily tasks with dignity.

Hallucination: A visual, auditory, or olfactory perception of something that's not there. Alzheimer's patients are prone to have hallucinations.

HIPAA: A document through which the dementia patients consent a third party to use or disclose their protected health information

Hippocampus: Part of the brain that generates short-term memory and emotions.

History: Medical and psycho-social history serve to detail previous treatments and incidents that the person has gone through, as to facilitate further treatment.

Huntington's Disease: A rare disease that causes involuntary movements and can develop into dementia. Huntington's disease appears in people between ages 30–45 years, and limits their life expectancy in fifteen more years.

Incontinence: Incapacity of controlling bladder and bowel functions. This is a common symptom in Alzheimer's patients, and can be treated in its early stages, though the use of geriatric diaper may become necessary.

Instrumental Activities of Daily Living (IADLs): Home management activities that improve people's lives in a community, though they are not as crucial as the ADLs. It includes housekeeping, financial management, preparing meals, getting around in a vehicle or public transportation, managing medicines, etc.

Intuitive thought processes: Thought process that happens in the right side of the brain, and which happens spontaneously and instantaneously, without requiring effort. Through the intuitive process, we get feelings, impressions, and instinctive responses, even if those contradict our rational feelings. Intuitive thought processes are fueled by our past experiences, and they allow us to enjoy art and beauty.

Korsakoff's Syndrome: Degenerative brain disease caused by alcohol abuse, which can affect short-term memory and make it hard to learn new skills.

Level of Care: Divided into mild (or "early"), moderate (or "middle"), and severe (or "late") this term reflects the amount of care that a person needs at a given point of their dementia treatment. The level of care is usually low at the moment of the diagnosis, but symptoms get worse as the disease progresses, and it's important to know when and how to get help.

<u>Lewy Body Dementia</u>: The second most common type of dementia, Lewy Body is caused by protein deposits in the nervous system, which affects memory, thinking, and movements. In late stages, the person suffers from visual hallucinations and symptoms associated with Parkinson's disease, such as tremors, rigid muscles, trouble walking, and slow movements.

<u>Living Will</u>: A document written and signed by a dementia patient after the diagnosis, but while they're still in control of their cognitive abilities. Through the living will, the dementia patient states their medical wishes and makes provisions for legal matters that may arise when they are not fully conscious anymore.

<u>Long Term Memory</u>: Memory that can be stored indefinitely, holding an unlimited amount of information.

<u>Mild Cognitive Impairment (MCI)</u>: A cognitive problem that can be perceived, but is not strong enough to have a harmful impact on a person's life.

<u>Mindfulness</u>: The basic human ability of being conscious of the world around, being present, and perceiving things around you. It can be achieved through meditation and mental exercises.

<u>Mindlessness</u>: The opposite of mindfulness—being unaware of what you're doing, making unconscious decisions because your mind is wandering.

<u>Magnetic Resonance Imaging (MRI)</u>: Radiology technique that uses body magnetism and computers to get images from inside the body, including the brain, which is valuable in dementia diagnosis and prognosis.

Muscle memory: The ability of remembering and repeating a task by following a pattern of movements without being conscious of it. Muscle memory is an enemy of mindfulness, and it can be broken by an unexpected situation that arises while you perform your task.

Neurodegenerative: Diseases that affect the structure and functioning of the brain tissue. Neurodegenerative diseases are more common in the elderly, but can show up in younger people.

Neurology: Medicine field that deals with the nervous system.

Occipital Lobe: Part of the brain that controls sight and the capacity of recognizing things. Located at the lower rear of the bran.

Paranoia: An acute feeling of suspicion without rational reasoning behind it.

Parietal Lobes: Part of the brain responsible for touch, pressure, pain, temperature, and taste. Located at the upper rear of the brain.

Parkinson's Disease: Neurological disorder that interferes with muscle, affecting gait and facial features, as well as causing tremors. Parkinson usually occurs during the early sixties, and moves slowly and progressively, and can cause symptoms of dementia.

Pathology: Field of medicine that studies diseases, establishing its causes, symptoms, and effects, by examining their impacts on the body.

Perception: Recognizing external stimuli through the five senses and interpreting them through an unconscious memory association.

<u>Person-Centered Care</u>: A type of dementia care that's based on each person's unique traits. The caregiver will take the person's life story and personality into account when planning and executing their activities, instead of following a pre-made formula.

<u>Pick's Disease</u>: Neurodegenerative disease that's a type of frontotemporal dementia, affecting the frontal and temporal lobes of the brain. It usually hits people between their 40' and 65's, first affecting the speech, then memory, and personality.

<u>Plaques & Tangles</u>: Interferences between the transmission of neurons, caused by Alzheimer's disease, preventing the neural system to exchange signals to each other. Plaques and tangles can only be identified during an autopsy.

<u>Psychosocial</u>: The psychological and social aspects related to a person's behavior.

<u>Psychotropic Drugs</u>: Drugs that have an effect on the brain, influencing a person's mental health. They can be antidepressant, anxiolytics, tranquilizers, and other drugs that have an effect on the patient's emotions and behavior.

<u>Rational Thought Processes</u>: These processes happen on the left side of the brain, and are responsible for methodical choices, interpretations, prioritizing actions and information, and following steps to achieve a goal. This kind of thought requires effort, and can tell us if we are having proper behavior during a situation, and how to act from there.

<u>Remembering-self</u>: A narrative used to make sense of our own history by reinterpreting nostalgic elements of ourselves to create a familiarity of our current surroundings.

<u>Strength-based care</u>: Treatment based on encouraging the use of the set of skills that a person continues to have while their dementia progresses. Knowing what these skills are helps care-

givers to develop activities for that person, which benefits their experience.

<u>Sundowning Syndrome</u>: Sensation of disorientation and irritability that some people with dementia have when the sun goes down at the end of the day. Its causes are not clear, but could have to do with the change in the environment or the feeling of tiredness.

<u>Temporal Lobes</u>: Part of the brain responsible for audition, also connected with memory, language, emotion, interpretation, and learning. Located above the ears.

<u>Vascular Dementia</u>: Type of dementia caused by several small strokes, which are often not perceived, but can have an impact in the brain.

<u>Wandering</u>: Moving around aimlessly without goal or direction, which can bring a person of dementia to exhaustion or take them to a place where their security is at risk. It's possible to wander safely if there's an appropriate space for that, such as a garden or a backyard.

<u>Ward of Court</u>: A person appointed by the court to manage the affairs of a dementia patient who has been declared legally incapable of doing that themselves

BIBLIOGRAPHY

Aarp, A. G. (n.d.). *Time management for the caregiver*. AARP. https://www.aarp.org/home-family/caregiving/info-2016/time-management-for-caregiver.html

Activities for dementia. (2021, December 8). nhs.uk. https://www.nhs.uk/conditions/dementia/activities/

Alzheimer's and dementia: Tips for better communication. (2021, March 12). Mayo Clinic. https://www.mayoclinic.org/healthy-lifestyle/caregivers/in-depth/alzheimers/art-20047540

Alzheimer's Disease: common medical problems. (n.d.). National Institute on Aging. https://www.nia.nih.gov/health/alzheimers-disease-common-medical-problems

Alzheimer's disease facts and figures. (n.d.). Alzheimer's Association. https://www.alz.org/alzheimers-dementia/facts-figures

Alzheimer's: Managing sleep problems. (2021, December 3). Mayo Clinic. https://www.mayoclinic.org/healthy-lifestyle/caregivers/in-depth/alzheimers/art-20047832

Alzheimer's Association. (2023). *10 Early Signs and Symptoms of Alzheimer's*. Retrieved from https://www.alz.org/alzheimers-dementia/10_signs

Alzheimer's Association. (2023). *Diagnosis of Alzheimer's Disease*. Retrieved from https://www.alz.org/alzheimers-dementia/diagnosis

Alzheimer's Association. (2023). *Legal documents*. Retrieved from https://www.alz.org/help-support/caregiving/financial-legal-planning/legal-documents

Alzheimer's Association. (2023). *Myths About Alzheimer's Disease*. Retrieved from https://www.alz.org/alzheimers-dementia/what-is-alzheimers/myths

Alzheimer's Association. (2023). *What Is Dementia?* Retrieved from https://www.alz.org/alzheimers-dementia/what-is-dementia

Alzheimer's Association. (2024). *Choosing a Doctor to Evaluate Memory and Thinking Problems*. Retrieved from https://www.alz.org/media/Documents/alzheimers-dementia-choosing-a-doctor-ts.pdf

Alzheimer's Association. (2023). *Questions for Your Doctor*. Retrieved from https://www.alz.org/alzheimers-dementia/treatments/questions-for-your-doctor

Alzheimer's Disease International (ADI). (2013). *Dementia-friendly Communities*. Alzheimer's Society. (2023). *Communicating with someone with dementia*

Alzheimer's Society. (2023). *Making your home dementia-friendly*. Retrieved from https://www.alzheimers.org.uk/get-support/staying-independent/what-equipment-improve-adapt-home-person-dementia

Alzheimer's Society. (2023). *Telling people about your dementia diagnosis.* Retrieved from https://www.alzheimers.org.uk/get-support/daily-living/telling-people-about-your-dementia-diagnosis

Alzheimer's Society. (2023). *Types of dementia.* Retrieved from https://www.alzheimers.org.uk/about-dementia/types-dementia

Alzheimer's Society. (2023). *Why get a diagnosis?*

The benefits of socialization for people with dementia | The Arbors - The Ivy. (2023, June 21). *The* Arbors & The Ivy Assisted Living. https://arborsassistedliving.com/the-benefits-of-socialization-for-people-with-dementia

Brodaty, H., & Arasaratnam, C. (2012). Meta-analysis of nonpharmacological interventions for neuropsychiatric symptoms of dementia. *American Journal of Psychiatry, 169*(10), 1020-1029.

Buckwalter, K. C., & Hall, G. R. (2002). *Geriatric mental health nursing.* Mosby.

Canevelli, M., Valletta, M., Trebbastoni, A., Sarli, G., D'Antonio, F., Tariciotti, L., ... & Bruno, G. (2016). Sundowning in dementia: Clinical relevance, pathophysiological determinants, and therapeutic approaches. *Frontiers in Medicine, 3,* 73.

Cohen, D., & Eisdorfer, C. (2002). *The loss of self: A family resource for the care of Alzheimer's disease and related disorders.* W. W. Norton & Company.

Communicating with someone with dementia. (2023, February 24). nhs.uk. https://www.nhs.uk/conditions/dementia/communication-and-dementia/

Communication and Alzheimer's. (n.d.). Alzheimer's Disease and Dementia. https://www.alz.org/help-support/caregiving/daily-care/communications

Coxwell, K. (2022). How to deal with dementia or Alzheimer's: 5 retirement financial planning steps. *NewRetirement.* https://www.newretirement.com/retirement/how-to-deal-with-dementia-or-alzheimers-5-retirement-financial-planning-steps/

Dementia. (2023, March 15). www.who.int. https://www.who.int/news-room/fact-sheets/detail/dementia

Dementia - activities and exercise. (n.d.). Better Health Channel. https://www.betterhealth.vic.gov.au/health/conditionsandtreatments/dementia-activities-and-exercise

Dementia - behavior changes. (n.d.). Better Health Channel. https://www.betterhealth.vic.gov.au/health/conditionsandtreatments/dementia-behaviour-changes

Dementia - hygiene. (n.d.). Better Health Channel. https://www.betterhealth.vic.gov.au/health/conditionsandtreatments/dementia-hygiene

Dementia - Symptoms and causes - Mayo Clinic. (2023, June 22). Mayo Clinic. https://www.mayoclinic.org/diseases-conditions/dementia/symptoms-causes/syc-20352013

Dementia: 7 stages. (n.d.). Compassion & Choices. https://www.compassionand choices.org/resource/dementia-7-stages

Dementia nurse interview questions and answers. (n.d.). https://fixedcareer.com/ dementia-nurse-interview-questions/

Dementia planning is an important part of estate planning. (2022, August 18). Moneyweb. https://www.moneyweb.co.za/financial-advisor-views/demen tia-planning-is-an-important-part-of-estate-planning/

Dementia Terminology. (2023, May 30). The Good Care Group. https://www. thegoodcaregroup.com/live-in-care/dementia-care/dementia-terminology/

DementiaCareCentral.com (2023, January 26). *Stages of Alzheimer's & dementia: Durations & scales used to measure progression (GDS, FAST & CDR).* www.de mentiacarecentral.com. https://www.dementiacarecentral.com/aboutdemen tia/facts/stages

Dementia-friendly communities. (n.d.). Alzheimer's Society. https://www. alzheimers.org.uk/get-involved/dementia-friendly-communities/

Dementia-friendly faith groups. (n.d.). Alzheimer's Society. https://www. alzheimers.org.uk/get-involved/dementia-friendly-communities/faith- groups

Dementia Terminology. (n.d.). The Good Care Group. https://www.thegoodcare group.com/live-in-care/dementia-care/dementia-terminology/

Doka, K. J. (1989). *Disenfranchised grief: Recognizing hidden sorrow.* Lexington Books.

Get involved with your local chapter. (n.d.). Alzheimer's Disease and Dementia. https://www.alz.org/local_resources/find_your_local_chapter

How to communicate with a person with dementia. (2021, December 20). Alzheimer's Society. https://www.alzheimers.org.uk/about-dementia/symp toms-and-diagnosis/symptoms/how-to-communicate-dementia

How to talk to the doctor about your elderly parent or spouse. (n.d.). © 2007-2023 AgingCare All Rights Reserved. https://www.agingcare.com/articles/ doctor-visits-with-elderly-parent-149071.htm

Kübler-Ross, E. (1969). *On death and dying.* Macmillan.

Legal documents. (n.d.). Alzheimer's Disease and Dementia. https://www.alz.org/ help-support/caregiving/financial-legal-planning/legal-documents

Lourida, I., Soni, M., Thompson-Coon, J., Purandare, N., Lang, I. A., Ukoumunne, O. C., ... & Llewellyn, D. J. (2019). Mediterranean diet, cognitive function, and dementia: a systematic review and meta-analysis. *The BMJ, 367,* l6882.

Lyketsos, C. G., Carrillo, M. C., Ryan, J. M., Khachaturian, A. S., Trzepacz, P., Amatniek, J., ... & Breitner, J. C. (2011). Neuropsychiatric symptoms in Alzheimer's disease. *Alzheimer's & Dementia, 7*(5), 532-539.

Mace, N. L., & Rabins, P. V. (2017). *The 36-Hour Day: A Family Guide to Caring for People Who Have Alzheimer Disease, Other Dementias, and Memory Loss.* Johns Hopkins University Press.

Marquand, B. (2023, March 20). *Long-term care insurance explained*. NerdWallet. https://www.nerdwallet.com/article/insurance/long-term-care-insurance

McKeith, I. G., Dickson, D. W., Lowe, J., Emre, M., O'Brien, J. T., Feldman, H., ... & Dubois, B. (2005). *Diagnosis and management of dementia with Lewy bodies: third report of the DLB Consortium*. Neurology, 65(12), 1863-1872.

Moniz-Cook, E., Vernooij-Dassen, M., & Woods, R. T. (2006). Non-pharmacological interventions for agitation in dementia: A systematic review. *The British Journal of Psychiatry, 188*(1), 34-42.

National Institute on Aging. (2021). *Getting a diagnosis*.

National Institute on Aging. (2021). *What are the signs and symptoms of dementia?*

National Institute on Aging. (2021). *What Happens to the Brain in Alzheimer's Disease?* Retrieved from https://www.nia.nih.gov/health/what-happens-brain-alzheimers-disease

National Institute on Aging. (2023). *Managing Money Problems for People With Dementia*. Retrieved from https://www.nia.nih.gov/health/legal-and-financial-planning/managing-money-problems-people-dementia

National Institute on Aging. (2024). *Caregiver Stress*.

National Institutes of Health (NIH). (2021). *Vascular contributions to cognitive impairment and dementia (VCID): A National Institute on Aging (NIA)-Alzheimer's Association (AA) Research Framework*. Alzheimer's & Dementia, 17(9), 1324-1338.

New drug for Alzheimer's slows down cognitive decline in key trial. (2022, September 28). [Video]. NBC News. https://www.nbcnews.com/health/aging/alzheimers-drug-slowed-progression-disease-phase-3-trial-rcna49689

Orman, A., & Tierney, M. C. (2018). Technology for people with dementia: Opportunities and challenges. *American Journal of Alzheimer's Disease & Other Dementias®, 33*(8), 487-494.

Rabins, P. V., Lyketsos, C. G., & Steele, C. D. (2006). *Practical dementia care*. Oxford University Press.

Rando, T. A. (1993). *Treatment of complicated mourning*. Research Press.

Riemersma-van der Lek, R. F., Swaab, D. F., Twisk, J., Hol, E. M., Hoogendijk, W. J., & Van Someren, E. J. (2008). Effect of bright light and melatonin on cognitive and noncognitive function in elderly residents of group care facilities: a randomized controlled trial. Journal of the American Medical Association, 299(22), 2642-2655._

Särkämö, T., Tervaniemi, M., Laitinen, S., Forsblom, A., Soinila, S., Mikkonen, M., ... & Hietanen, M. (2008). Music listening enhances cognitive recovery and mood after middle cerebral artery stroke. *Brain, 131*(3), 866-876.

Self-Care for caregivers. (2022, June 24). ucsfhealth.org. https://www.ucsfhealth.org/education/self-care-for-caregivers

Shulman, E. (2017). *Before and after loss: A neurologist's perspective on loss, grief, and our brain*. W. W. Norton & Company.

Sleep issues and sundowning. (n.d.). Alzheimer's Disease and Dementia. https://

www.alz.org/help-support/caregiving/stages-behaviors/sleep-issues-
sundowning

Snyder, C. R. (2002). Hope theory: Rainbows in the mind. *Psychological Inquiry,
13*(4), 249-275.

Sollitto, M. (n.d.). *3 Legal documents caregivers need to manage a senior's health care.*
AgingCare. https://www.agingcare.com/articles/legal-documents-to-make-
healthcare-decisions-for-your-parent-146623.htm

Sorensen, S., Duberstein, P., Gill, D., & Pinquart, M. (2006). The factor structure
of caregiver burden in caregivers of persons with dementia. *Aging & Mental
Health, 10*(5), 511-519.

Support groups. (n.d.). Alzheimer's Disease and Dementia. https://www.alz.org/
help-support/community/support-groups

Taking care of you: Self-care for family caregivers - Family Caregiver Alliance. (2023,
January 11). Family Caregiver Alliance. https://www.caregiver.org/
resource/taking-care-you-self-care-family-caregivers/

The 10 benefits of early diagnosis. (n.d.). Alzheimer Society of Canada. https://
alzheimer.ca/en/about-dementia/do-i-have-dementia/how-get-tested-
dementia/10-benefits-early-diagnosis

Van Hook, M. (2022, March 26). *Making a dementia care plan: 10 questions to ask
your doctor.* The Arbor Company. https://www.arborcompany.com/blog/
making-dementia-care-plan-10-questions-to-ask

Van der Steen, J. T., Smaling, H. J., De Lange, J., Van Achterberg, T., & Jansen, B.
(2014). The effect of creative activities on quality of life in dementia patients:
A systematic review. *The British Journal of Psychiatry, 205*(1), 15-20._

Vernooij-Dassen, M. J. F. J., Lousberg, R., Verhey, F. R. J., & Jansen, P. D. (2003).
Non-pharmacological interventions for agitation in dementia: A review of
the literature. *Geriatrics & Gerontology International, 3*(3), 149-157._

Waters, S. (2022, September 7). *6 self-care tips for caregivers.* Better Up. https://
www.betterup.com/blog/self-care-for-caregivers

What are frontotemporal disorders? Causes, symptoms, and treatment. (n.d.). National
Institute on Aging. https://www.nia.nih.gov/health/what-are-frontotempo
ral-disorders

What are the seven stages of dementia? | IP Homecare. (2021, October 12). IP Home-
care. https://www.ip-live-in-care.co.uk/7-stages-dementia/

What is a geriatric care manager? (n.d.). National Institute on Aging. https://www.
nia.nih.gov/health/what-geriatric-care-manager

What is a living trust? (2022, September 16). https://www.investopedia.com/
terms/l/living-trust.asp

What is Alzheimer's? (n.d.). Alzheimer's Disease and Dementia. https://www.alz.
org/alzheimers-dementia/what-is-alzheimers

What is dementia? (n.d.). Alzheimer's Disease and Dementia. https://www.alz.
org/alzheimers-dementia/what-is-dementia

What is dementia? | CDC. (n.d.). https://www.cdc.gov/aging/dementia/index.html

What is dementia? Symptoms, types, and diagnosis. (n.d.). National Institute on Aging. https://www.nia.nih.gov/health/what-is-dementia

What Is Lewy Body dementia? Causes, symptoms, and treatments. (n.d.). National Institute on Aging. https://www.nia.nih.gov/health/what-lewy-body-dementia-causes-symptoms-and-treatments

What is mixed dementia? (n.d.). Alzheimer's Society. https://www.alzheimers.org.uk/blog/what-is-mixed-dementia

What not to say to somebody with dementia. (n.d.). Alzheimer's Society. https://www.alzheimers.org.uk/blog/language-dementia-what-not-to-say

Williams, K. N., & Tappen, R. M. (2014). *Geriatric nursing.* F. A. Davis Company.

Yang, X., Vedel, I., & Khanassov, V. (2021). The Cultural Diversity of Dementia Patients and Caregivers in Primary Care Case Management: a Pilot Mixed Methods Study. *Canadian Geriatrics Journal, 24*(3), 184–194. https://doi.org/10.5770/cgj.24.490

www.ingramcontent.com/pod-product-compliance
Lightning Source LLC
Chambersburg PA
CBHW071323140726

47996CB00005B/1797